Kern and Burn

**Conversations With
Design Entrepreneurs**

D1166694

Kern and Burn

Conversations With
Design Entrepreneurs

Tim Hoover
Jessica Karle Heltzel

Kern and Burn: Conversations With Design Entrepreneurs

ISBN 978-0-9891832-0-8

First Edition

Copy Editor: Allison Loerch

Designers: Tim Hoover and Jessica Karle Heltzel

Cover Illustration: The Heads of State

Printed and bound: Shapco Printing, Minnesota

Paper: Mohawk Via Pure White Smooth

Typefaces:

Graphik, Commercial Type; Christian Schwartz, 2009

Adelle, Type Together; José Scaglione, Veronika Burian, 2009

For those who kern, those who burn
and those who embrace the risk of failure daily.

Contents

Illustrations

Foreword

Keenan Cummings

I

I graduated from design school with boundless optimism, jumping from the bubble of university life into a post-recession real world, where hope was a rare commodity. I believed that design could induce change—that it could shape the way we understand and interact with our world.

I moved to New York for a lead design position at a two-person shop and considered myself lucky to be employed, even though we didn't have a single client. We filled our time with small-scale side projects that we hoped would land us paying jobs. The projects did lead to new clients, and the cash started rolling in.

For the first time in my career, I felt like a legitimate designer—but I wasn't challenged; I was comfortable. I left my first job for an in-house position at a large corporation, and my optimism quickly turned to cynicism. I realized that I didn't want to be handed a creative brief with a prescribed set of constraints. I wanted to discover and define the problems, develop the constraints, and build the processes that would lead to a deeper level of problem solving. I wanted to be credited and accountable for every part of the process. I wanted to build things that were a little less perfect, but more fully mine.

I knew that an alternate universe was out there—one that defied my experience—I just needed to find the path.

II

In creative work, we often talk about several kinds of seeing. We learn observation: We notice and synthesize interesting or inspiring things that easily can be passed over. We master inspection, focusing and refining down to the tiniest details. We practice perception, the human side of observing, which is a mix of noticing and empathy. But there's an illusive type of seeing we refer to as vision—the ability to see beyond the current context and, almost tangibly, sense possible futures.

I wanted to do more meaningful work, but found myself wandering. I had no clear vision for what my possible future could look like. The only way I could hope to make out the horizon was through relentless iteration.

So that's what I did.

I jumped into another job and tried my hand at many roles. I started side projects. I launched blogs, wire-framed products, drafted business plans, and did case studies on existing products that I wanted to improve. I went to events, took evening classes, met people for advice and feedback, often harsh.

I failed several interviews and collaborated with new-found friends. I felt around in the dark, but it was better than sitting comfortably waiting for a light to turn on. After six months of struggling and grasping to find the right path, I met a cofounder and built a company that makes me incredibly proud. In one stroke, everything appeared to fall neatly into place. In reality, it was more of a beginning than an end, and there was nothing neat about it. A week after I decided to leave my stable job — a steady paycheck, benefits and opportunities waiting for me up the chain — my wife gave birth to our son.

Despite new and extraordinary life changes, I left behind all options for the path I chose. In a single year, I built my company and developed the most important thing in my career — a vision for my work.

III

Steve Jobs said, "When you grow up, you tend to get told that the world is the way it is, and [you just live your life] inside the world, try not to bash into the walls too much, try to have a nice family life, have fun, save a little money. That's a very limited life. Life can be much broader, once you discover one simple fact, and this is, everything around you that you call life was made up by people that were no smarter than you. And you can change it, you can influence it, you can build your own things that other people can use. Once you learn that, you'll never be the same again."

I discovered the real opportunity for designers is to not only shape the world and decide its path, but to provide ways for others to do the same.

This book is an ode to creators and builders, those who have found their vision and pursued it with force. What these entrepreneurs have in common is that deep down, in their hearts and bones, there's something a bit spiritual that stirs them. It moves mouse and mind, and it produces pixels and poetry.

We put tools into the hands of improbable artists, helping them build communities and connections, and chart paths that encourage creativity and foster influence.

These unlikely makers come from all corners of the world and have diverse backgrounds and upbringings, but the products we create provide ways for them to reach beyond their immediate context and tell stories about the people they want to be — not just the people circumstances have decided they are. There's a moment when they, too, can come to believe their work might, in some small way, influence how others see and interact with their environment. As developers of these tools, communities and pathways, we get to design that moment and shape the world.

Introduction

In 1957, seven of the world's top scientists, engineers and physicists set out to convince Robert Noyce—a brilliant 29-year-old Midwestern physicist—to leave their jobs at Shockley Semiconductor Laboratory and join them in a new business venture. These seven men were some of the best minds in electronics, and they knew their collective abilities far outweighed the opportunities presented to them at Shockley, a Palo Alto, Calif.-based company that built transistors and was started by Nobel Prize-winning physicist William Shockley. They also knew they needed Noyce to lead them.

Noyce was hesitant.

Mid-20th Century American culture encouraged young, aspiring employees like Noyce to put in their time, climb the corporate ladder and eventually retire from the same company in which they started. They were taught to believe in the ideas and vision of their employer. Hierarchy was king and traditional values celebrated loyalty. Risk and entrepreneurship were reserved for the privileged few.

When Noyce's attempts to convince his colleagues to stay at Shockley failed, he joined them, and the group announced their plans to quit. They received a letter from their superiors that read:

"This is a shameful act, you need to consider the consequences. You have essentially turned traitor. You have broken what everyone knows is the contract that you make when you start working at a company, which is: You're there forever. You've changed the rules of the game and you're never gonna live that down."

The group's decision to leave Shockley was unprecedented. They looked for outside financing and charged forward into the unknown world of entrepreneurship, with trust in their brilliant minds and one another. They gave up security and a consistent paycheck to build products and a company based on their own ideas and beliefs—and earned a new moniker, the "Traitorous Eight."

Sherman Fairchild—an inventor, serial entrepreneur and son of IBM's cofounder, George Winthrop Fairchild—came to the group's aid as their financial backer. They founded Fairchild Semiconductor, commonly known as America's first venture-backed startup. In a few short but unpredictable years, under Noyce's leadership, Fairchild grew to become the leading producer of technology—in what was then known as the Santa Clara valley—and nurtured employees who founded more than 100 of their own companies, called Fairchildren, over the next 20 years.

One of the Fairchildren, started by Noyce and another one of the Traitorous Eight, Gordon

Moore, opened in 1967 under the name Intel. Based on Noyce's original integrated circuit innovations, Intel developed memory devices and went on to create the world's first commercial microprocessor chip in 1971. Santa Clara Valley became known as Silicon Valley, and our world changed forever.

More than 40 years later, we live in what Robert Safian describes as a place where the future of business is chaotic and impossible to predict. Employees no longer sign up to work for companies for their entire careers — they work in uncertain economic times; they watch as traditional institutions struggle to find new structures to fend off disruptors, and they listen to warnings of a dim future.

In his article for *Fast Company*, "This Is Generation Flux: Meet The Pioneers Of The New (And Chaotic) Frontier Of Business," Safian writes, "When businesspeople search for the right forecast—for the road map and model that will define the next era—no credible long-term picture emerges. There is one certainty, however. The next decade or two will be defined more by fluidity than by any new, settled paradigm; if there is a pattern to all of this, it is that there is no pattern."

Safian calls those who succeed under the pressures of today's conditions Generation Flux. "What defines GenFlux," he says, "is a mind-set that embraces instability, that tolerates—and even enjoys—recalibrating careers, business models, and assumptions." The "status quo" is an obsolete framework for innovation, so there is little choice but to invent new ways of doing things. And invention is no longer reserved for the world's best and brightest scientists, physicists and engineers.

It took Shockley Semiconductor Laboratory to bring together eight minds that forever changed our world, but today the Internet has connected us all. We have the tools to collaborate, to educate ourselves and to build the things we want for our lives — we are the inventors of our day.

Online learning communities, crowdfunding platforms and social media outlets have removed barriers and increased the ways people can define and share their stories. In today's world, it takes a well-told story to rise to the top—one that connects the dots for us in new ways—and designers are well-suited authors.

These digital tools have broken down geographic boundaries. Billions of people access and connect to an overwhelming amount of information daily, and they search for ways to parse through the chaos.

In his blog post "Dear Graphic and Web Designers please understand that there are greater opportunities available to you," Ben Pieratt writes: "The Internet, at this time in history, is the greatest client assignment of all time. The Western world is porting itself over to the web in mind and deed and is looking to make itself comfortable and productive. It's every person in the world, connected to every other person in the world, and no one fully understands how to make best use of this new reality because no one has seen anything like it before. The Internet wants to hire you to build stuff for it because it's trying to figure out what it can do. It's offering you a blank check and asking you to come up with something fascinating and useful that it can embrace en masse, to the benefit of everyone."

Today's designers are equipped with the skills necessary for critical thinking, empathy and powerful storytelling. They are trained to identify problems and invent solutions. No longer a sign of treason, entrepreneurship is essential. Those who do it best are not ostracized but are held in high esteem.

This book celebrates these design entrepreneurs. We interviewed 30 individuals who embrace uncertainty and take risks. These designers manufacture products, start side projects, self-publish books and found startups. They ask themselves important, hard questions and use design to discover the answers. These designers are seasoned veterans, Internet sensations, and self-taught young guns— but their résumés and degrees are not why we chose them. We chose them because they hustle; they are passionate, and they have a perspective. They are fully equipped for success in today's self-made environment.

The designers in this book might not have been invited into Robert Noyce's inner circle four decades ago but they channel the Traitorous Eights' spirit. They are like us. They are brilliant because they have the audacity to try. They took an idea they had at the bar, in the shower or at the office, and figured out how to make it happen. Whether they grew an idea slowly as a side project, or quit their jobs and raised capital, they all embraced the risk of failure. They boldly moved toward an uncertain future and made their dreams a reality.

Celebrate them, for they have made it a little bit easier for the rest of us. Our hope is that we can learn from them—not to follow in their footsteps, but to chart our own course in parallel, one that allows us to thrive, add value to the world and love what we do.

We all have a decision to make. We can put our time in and hope to be promoted, decorated or noticed. We can retire from the same company that we sign up for, or, we can take matters into our own hands, invite our talented friends along for the journey, and run as fast as we can into the unknown. There is no better time than now.

The Fairchild / Shockley 8, Fairchild Headquarters; Photo, © Wayne Miller / Magnum Photos

USA. 1960. The Fairchild/Shockley 8, who left the lab of Nobel Prize winner William Shockley to form Silicon Valley's first startup, Fairchild Semiconductor.
From left: Gordon Moore, C. Sheldon Roberts, Eugene Kleiner, Robert Noyce, Victor Grinich, Julius Blank, Jean Hoerni and Jay Last.

Conversations

Ben Pieratt | Cofounder, Svpply | New York, NY

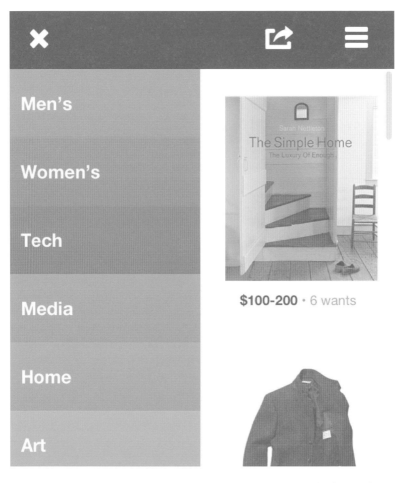

Svpply, iPhone Application

"Designers have the ability to disrupt billion
dollar markets. It's happening all around us."

Ben Pieratt

Take Greater Opportunities

Ben Pieratt has a passion for devouring the web. He experiments with, tears down and builds up new business models, and his passion for contributing to the web community is as vibrant as ever. He is the cofounder of Svpply, a new kind of online retail platform that curates products. He collaborates with companies such as Fictive Kin to shape the identity and product design of such applications as Rushmore and Done Not Done.

His transparent, inspirational writing has moved many designers, including ourselves, to realize the greater opportunities available to them and take the first step toward pursuing their passions.

What is your background, and how did you come to design?

I grew up in Brazil and moved back to the U.S. during my senior year of high school. It wasn't a great year, and I spent a lot of it locked away in my bedroom, messing around with Photoshop and devouring the web on the Graphite iMac that my parents bought for me. I loved that thing. I took my senior portrait with it. I visited one of my brothers at college and saw a still life he'd drawn of a bunch of doughnuts he'd pinned to the wall—that drawing was honestly one of the main reasons I went to art school for my freshman year of college—it was that or psychology.

Geocities and portfolio websites were a big deal for me. I built and tore down a lot of useless experiments over the course of the next few years. I miss a lot of aspects about that era of the web—experimental websites with ambience and no real express purpose. I had a lot of heroes back then whose careers I still follow today, such as Mike Cina, Mike Young, GMunk, Cuban Council, Folkert Gorter from Newstoday and Thomas Brody from Surfstation. I remember the first time my portfolio was featured on Surfstation. I just about died. I made some great friends through online communities during that time and ultimately started my first design studio with them right out of college in 2004.

Your blog post, 'Dear Graphic and web Designers, please understand that there are greater opportunities available to you' is a huge inspiration to us and was one of the catalysts for our desire to share the stories of those who design careers for themselves. What was your main motivation for writing the post?

I was lucky enough to be chosen by the market for an amazing opportunity that put me in a different position than a lot of people in this industry. I wanted to communicate that there is an emerging industry available for designers to consider, and that I was vouching for its merit.

You wrote an equally inspiring post titled, 'I have no idea what I'm doing.' Do you think the Internet has allowed design leaders to be more authentic with their companies and publish things before they are perfect?

We act more transparently because the availability of information online is giving us no choice but to shift our behavior in a way that makes this new fact feel normal. There's nothing noble about pursuing new levels of transparency; we're keeping pace with a new reality that few of us realized we were volunteering for. This kind of stuff leaks out into the culture in all sorts of unexpected ways, such as CEOs publicly discussing their failings, and reality television.

At what point did realize that your design talent could do more than execute other people's ideas and create 'nice logos and some nice websites?'

It was around the same time that I started to understand the potential of Svpply. It's a strange thing to sit around a table with smart people and seriously discuss disrupting billion dollar markets. But it's plausible, and after awhile, the horizons in your head expand, and you start to take it as a given that designers have the ability to disrupt billion dollar markets because it's happening all around us, by people just like us.

You seem to understand that being a designer is as much about empathy with users and being thoughtful as it is about technique and pixel pushing. What are some key qualities that designers should develop to prepare to cofound companies or to work in the startup world?

If a designer wants to cofound a company, my advice for them is to develop an understanding and a peace with what they want.

Ask yourself, 'Do you want to be a great business leader, or do you want to be a great designer?' If it's your first go-around at something like this, then chances are you might not be able to tackle both. If you want to be the best UX designer in the world, then concentrate on that. Don't let your ego and your thirst for experience distract you into thinking your opinion needs to be heard at the same level as your cofounder's on all topics, such as hiring, copywriting, product scheduling, business relationships, etc. Steve Jobs and Mark Zuckerberg are a poison in this regard.

Can you give a summary of Svpply's mission and the opportunity you saw in the market that it fulfills?

Svpply started as a social window-shopping experiment. As it grew in size, we saw more clearly how we were aggregating interest in products, and how valuable that kind of information could be for the retail supply chain.

For instance, if I'm a T-shirt boutique, and I have two shirts on Svpply, one with 650 people who 'Want' it and one with 20, then not only do I know which shirt I should print more of, I know that I have an audience to sell it to.

The opportunity lies in building a more efficient, rewarding communications channel between consumers and makers.

How did you find a technology partner for Svpply? What advice can you give a designer who needs to find a developer to work with?
I got lucky. I made a good friend, Eric Jacobsen, early on in my career. We met through an aforementioned online forum, where I asked for help with some code issues I was having with my parents' website. I have no advice on this because I haven't had to go through it. Hustle and make some friends, hey?

Designers are now encouraged by many to cofound startups. What is the best method for designers to become educated in business? Is it something best learned outside of academia, through experience?
The only way I've learned is through experience, but I wouldn't say that's an endorsement. I sometimes wish I'd spent time working at a startup or a well-managed studio before going out on my own, but I can't necessarily say that it would have been the better route. The only advice I can give is to listen as hard as you can to the advice of people in your life whom you respect.

What do you find most exciting about the interconnectivity of the whole world on the Internet?
Ha. I find it incredible that the technological groundwork for massive new means of commerce and communication are already in place, and the only holdup is our inventiveness and cultural willingness to embrace change.

SVPPLY

Svpply, Logo

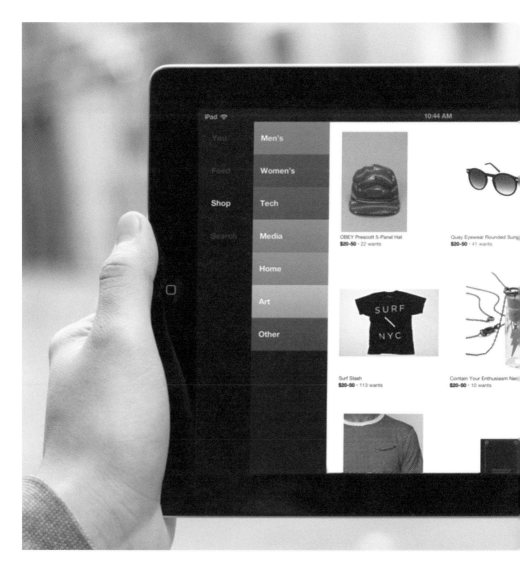

Svpply, iPad Application

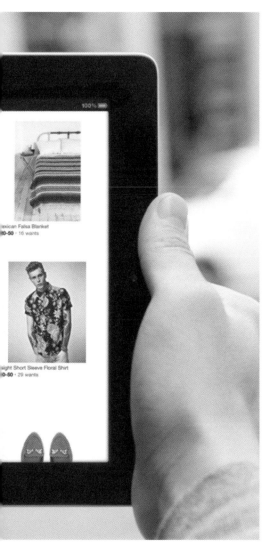

What is the biggest risk you've taken in your career? What failures are you thankful for?
I'm a Western, white male with a lot of people in my life who love me. The worst thing that happens to me is I file for bankruptcy and ask my in-laws if we can move our family into their basement for a while. The worst-case scenario in my life is so privileged that I think it's disingenuous to call anything I do risky. I'm not especially thankful for any of my failures yet.

Do you have any additional advice for talented designers who have entrepreneurial ambitions but aren't sure where to start or are unfamiliar with the startup world?
I've only done this dance once, but from what I see, these steps should work:
Figure out what you want to build.

If you don't know what you want to build, then start paying closer attention to the things that already interest you. Get it built and launched.

Money isn't going to introduce you to a technical cofounder, and no investor is going to give you money as a designer with an idea, so find someone to build it with, get it built, and launch that mother. I know that's not helpful at all, but you're just going to have to figure out how to get that part done.

If you see interesting growth, the rest will take care of itself.

Cameron Koczon | Cofounder, Fictive Kin | Brooklyn, NY

Rushmore.fm, Online Music Community

"Designers need to be in the mix from the beginning,
 and currently, this is rarely the case."

Cameron Koczon

Make Something You Love

Cameron Koczon does not consider himself a designer. Yet, as a cofounder of Fictive Kin, the web conference Brooklyn Beta and web applications such as TeuxDeux and Gimme Bar, he has become an integral part of the creative community in New York. He urges designers to seize opportunities, become partners and search for realignment.

He outlines the path to change through designer-cofounded startups, side projects and projects that tackle serious problems beyond the insular design community. He might not be a designer by title, but he understands the power of good design.

Have you always wanted to be in ownership of your work?
Yeah, I sort of knew that was the way it was going to be right out of the gates.

Did you know that you wanted to collaborate with creatives?
No. Not even entirely sure what that means. If you mean designers, the answer probably just stays no. I only recently started fiddling around with design. It took until after college for me to start getting properly stuck into the worlds of product design and front-end development.

You went to business school at Stanford. When was your first 'aha moment' when you realized the importance of design?
It didn't happen at business school. I guess I just sort of fell into design more than anything. I went from not really even knowing 'design' was a thing to giving it nearly my full attention. For whatever reason, my gateway drug ended up being grids, which I got turned onto by Khoi Vinh and Mark Boulton. I think I was especially attracted to them because they made design seem more like engineering than art. This made the discipline feel more accessible to me. I felt like design was something that could have almost mathlike solutions. Turns out I was wrong, but that's pretty close to how it got started.

Once you incorporated design into your work, did you find that it made an impact?

Yes. I think everyone who earnestly incorporates design into their work probably feels that way.

You feel strongly that designers should be cofounders; why?

Well, the language I tend to use is that designers should be 'partners.' In the startup world, that tends to mean that they should be cofounders. I believe this because I think designers need to be in the mix from the beginning, and currently, this is rarely the case. Design is way behind other disciplines when it comes to the world of web products. It's also worth noting that I do not think all designers should be CEOs. Running a company is a very different job, and it's not one that all designers will be good at, or would even want to do.

When you don't involve design from the beginning, other people, developers and business types, end up making design decisions without even really knowing it. These decisions later become constraints that the actual designer has to work around.

It's vaguely like sending a construction crew to lay down the foundation for a house and then calling an architect six months later to get them to design a home on it. They can do it, but you might not get the same home you would have if you'd started with just the plot of land.

MICA's GD MFA and SVA's Designer as Author + Entrepreneur graduate programs challenge the traditional design school model and push students toward self-generated content and self-initiated projects. Do designers need a graduate-level education to go out on their own?

Maybe. I don't know. I've gone back and forth a lot on this question, both as it pertains to designers and as it pertains to people who want to start businesses and whether they

Done Not Done, List Application

should get MBAs. I think it's more a question of personal path than anything else. Grad programs can be a great way to gather one's thoughts while learning essential skills, but they're also super expensive. I feel like really great stories could be told about both going to such a program or bypassing it for more of a self-taught, experiential route.

I would say that if you do go to a grad program, it's smart to know exactly why you are going, why you've chosen that specific program, and what exactly you expect to get out of it.

Do this in concrete terms. Saying you're going to 'learn things' isn't concrete. You need something you can objectively measure, so you can have a sense for what value you're trying to get for your time and money.

Should designers get a business education on top of the design knowledge?

It depends on what you want to do and what you want to be professionally. Ask yourself, 'Do I want to be a manager of people, or do I want to be a designer of things?'

There's nothing wrong with extra knowledge. If you define education as reading up on a subject, then it seems like a smart thing to do. Read stuff such as Paul Graham's essays or Guy Kawasaki's, *The Art of the Start* or *Getting Real* by 37 Signals. If you mean formal education, I'd guess that most designers could skip it.

Do you think designers are more accessible than developers in terms of finding great people to partner and work with?

I don't think that's true. There's a shortage of both good designers and good developers. Neither is especially accessible.

How can designers find great developers? How would you recommend doing it?

I'm curious, what do you think? I have some ideas, but I want to know what you think.

We feel like most partnerships just happen through who you meet or who you know.

That's not good. Then the advice becomes, 'Get lucky. Just try to stand in the right spot at the right moment when a developer is available.' I think a better plan, starting from no connections to developers, would be to just go to as many developer meetups as possible. I wouldn't talk about my idea for a while. I would just go out for drinks with everyone and connect one-on-one on a human level before I presented anything I was working on. Basically, make friends before you talk business.

You've often said that designers should develop an idea as far as they can before they pitch it.

I think that is a good idea. If you want to persuade a developer to believe that your project is important and something that he or she wants to be a part of, a key part of that is helping them visualize the idea.

The translation from idea to believable idea can be done really well with design. It can be really difficult with words. If you create a beautiful design solution for the problem you want to solve, you automatically check a bunch of boxes. One, you show the developer or investor that you know how to work. Two, you show your level of design skills.

Of course, this puts you in a vulnerable spot because you're going to be judged, face-to-face, on your abilities. But you should be able to handle that.

How has being part of Studiomates helped your career?

A great deal. At this point, Studiomates has done as much to shape my life as it has my career. It's the home of my New York family and the reason that things such as Brooklyn Beta and TeuxDeux exist. Not that I would have done nothing without it. I just would have done very different things.

How important is it to be known for a product or a project, in terms of opportunities?

When you are just getting started in an industry, I think it is probably quite important. This is especially true when meeting new folks. It becomes like a competency shortcut that lets people know something about you, your abilities, the kinds of things you like to work on, etc. Pointing people to some of your output is also a lot more natural and socially acceptable than trying to describe yourself and your abilities. Saying, 'I love simple design,' isn't really saying a whole lot, but pointing to something simple that you built does and it does so in a nice way. For me, it turned out to be helpful that someone could introduce me and say, 'Hey, this is Cameron; he worked on TeuxDeux.'

If they knew what that was, we'd have a lot of free context and backstory to work from in terms of hanging out and getting along. If you're out in the wild at a place such as SXSW or some other event, and you want to connect with people, it's quite nice if you've made something that they know about, even if it's just a list app.

Why did you and Tina Roth Eisenberg (SwissMiss) decide to create TeuxDeux?

It was a spur-of-the-moment thing. I had just recently moved to New York. I was working with Tina out of a space that would eventually become Studiomates, Tina was using a pen-and-paper analogue version of roughly the timeline view you see on the app. One day, she came back in to grab that week's paper to-do list, which she had almost forgotten. I said to her, 'That's how you keep track of what you need to do? We're web people! Let's make a web version. You design that, and we'll build it.' She designed it in a day, and Evan and I built it in a weekend. There was no strategy at all. It was a lot of fun. At least, that's how I think it happened. It was so spur of the moment that it's a little hard to remember exactly.

Brooklyn Beta is a web conference that you started with the aim to inspire people to make something they love. Did you plan to create a community or environment unique to Brooklyn?

Not really. BB is about inspiring designers and developers to work together as partners to make something they love. We often call it a conference for the 'work hard and be nice to people crowd.' There's no reason why it needs to be unique to Brooklyn. I think that would hurt its mission if folks felt they couldn't participate if they weren't in BK.

Of course, we do celebrate Brooklyn and its culture, food and history during the conference because it's our home, and we want to show it off a little bit.

We really hope that people leave the conference and say, 'There's a designer in this room, and there's a developer in this room; let's get together and make a product.' We want people to tackle bigger problems. Then they can take that with them back to wherever they're from and hopefully act on it.

Not insular design-centric projects...

That'd be my personal preference, though there's nothing wrong with doing the fun stuff for peers. That's just not really what the conference is about.

Do you want to set Brooklyn apart from the startup culture of Silicon Valley?

Not especially. Also, Brooklyn doesn't need my help to set itself apart with an identity all its own. I think it even has a distinct culture from a lot of the startup, product world in Manhattan. Brooklyn seems like a place full of product people but devoid of capital.

Would be great to see more capital make its way this direction, which is starting to happen now, as opposed to anyone in Brooklyn who wants to build a company needing to go into Manhattan to learn those cultural norms, etc.

Brooklyn Beta, Conference Website

You took the matchmaking idea even further by starting BB Summer Camp and removed the biggest barrier of all, money. You provide early funding to designer-developer teams. What was the process like working with the teams you eventually chose, and what's next for them and the conference?

All our teams are currently out doing their own fundraising. We partnered up with Craig Shapiro and the other lovely people at the Collaborative Fund, and consequently, our campers had a little more capital to survive post-Summer. Now they're fending for themselves and trying to get actual sustainable businesses going. On the whole, Summer Camp was a ton of fun but a lot more work than we expected. Really glad we did it. We're not yet sure what is next for either Summer Camp or the Brooklyn Beta conference. We are still figuring it all out. Not easy questions.

Beyond helping companies get their start through BB, Fictive Kin has partnered with betaworks to help build web products. Why partner, and why betaworks?

We partnered with them so that we can focus ruthlessly on building products, something we do well, while entrusting betaworks with the work of growing those products into great teams and companies, one of the many things they do well.

Fictive Kin has changed a lot over the years, but it's had one constant — a focus on good people above all else. We want to love what we do, but more importantly, we want to love whom we do it with. A 'fictive kin' is someone you think of as family even though you aren't actually related.

A looming problem with this approach, that we were doing our best to ignore, is that family doesn't scale very well. As companies grow, it becomes increasingly difficult to have a personal relationship with everyone in the organization.

At the same time, scale is necessary to have a big impact on the world. This tension between maintaining a small, close-knit team and doing something meaningful is a strong one, but it gets eliminated with this partnership. Fictive Kin can stay small and product-focused because we can trust the scaling to a team that is already great at that.

We wouldn't do a deal like this with anyone but betaworks. We've gotten to know their whole team, and in getting to know them and the work that they've done, we've found both an inspiration and a kindred spirit. We have complete faith in their ability to build and scale businesses because they've done it again and again. They know the Fictive Kin style of product development because they pioneered it. That also means there is a ton we can learn from them. Lastly, and most importantly, we think it's going to be a whole lot of fun to work with them, and we're convinced that they are the peanut butter to our jelly, or the peanut butter to our chocolate, or the peanut butter to our anything; the combination far outpaces what either can do on its own.

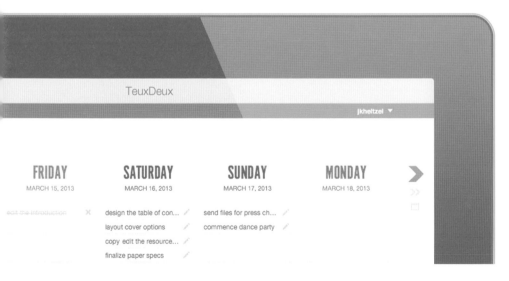

TeuxDeux, List Application

Randy J. Hunt | Creative Director, Etsy | Brooklyn, NY

Etsy Holiday Shop, Window; Art Direction and Design, Jeremy Perez-Cruz; Photo, Sara Kerens

"The desire to connect and be part of experiences that are shared and larger than ourselves is an innate part of being human."

Randy J. Hunt

Design and Build

Randy J. Hunt knows how to build meaningful connections and relationships. He cofounded Supermarket, a curated design marketplace, and currently is the creative director at Etsy — an even larger, community-focused online marketplace and resource for many aspiring entrepreneurs — where he leads a team of designers to build web products and create off-line experiences.

He also believes that designers must be able to build what they design. For Randy, to build is to make. With products such as Supermarket and Etsy, he builds so that others can make.

Can you tell us a little bit about your background and your path to design?
I first got into design through music. I was playing in bands and designing things such as T-shirts, fliers, CD covers, etc. I didn't really understand that it was design or that design was a profession, until I started to investigate the people who had designed records that I thought were awesome. I went to college and wanted to learn how to make software instruments. Along the way I took some required art classes and fell in love with screen printing, letterpress printing and book-binding.

In parallel, I was lucky enough to land a job with a boutique design studio that happened to be one of the few edgy design shops in Orlando, Fla. Most of what I learned about graphic design and typography I learned during my time spent there.

You attended SVA's MFA Designer as Entrepreneur program. In today's 'teach yourself' environment, is it necessary for designers to get graduate degrees?
I'm a boatload of contradictions in this regard. I absolutely loved graduate school, but I don't think it's necessary for designers to get graduate degrees — or degrees at all. I'd happily hire anyone for my team today regardless of their formal education background. A student should know what he or she wants to get out

of a formal education. Learning is the responsibility of the student. If anyone thinks that school happens, and then magically all is better in the world, they're severely misguided.

What can grad school provide? A safe place to experiment. A controlled environment where you meet peers with shared interests. A support system. You can find these things other places, and you can invent them yourself. For some people, some of the time, a formal education environment is great for that. For others, they might not need or want it. It was through SVA that I found my design family—both peers and incredible mentors. I couldn't have formed the same relationships any other way. I'm lucky to count among my friends and advisers extremely talented and experienced people I'd admired for so long.

You've said that you feel strongly that designers must be able to build what they design. Why?
More than anything I believe this speaks to an inquisitive mind and a desire to make the most well-made things one can. By 'build,' I loosely mean 'to make,' as in learn how to code a web application, learn how to print a design you're designing for print, and not be limited to renderings and mock-ups. By learning 'how to build' a few things happen:

You learn how tools work, what they are capable of and how to exploit them. You learn what it takes to build things, and can therefore better empathize with and appreciate those who are expert builders. You extend the potential influence of design. You can kick-start a building process, learn about the challenges your design decisions impose on the building process, and otherwise iterate on design throughout the building process.

It helps design move from being only at the front-end—planning—or only at the back-end—polish—and empowers the designer. As a person potentially naïve to the vocabulary,

Supercorp, Tote Bag

rules, mechanics and tools of 'building,' you can bring an interesting perspective to the process. There's a chance that you can contribute to the larger conversation in a novel way. Being able to build isn't the same as building everything all the time. It doesn't imply that you shouldn't work with other people who might be master builders. Nor does it mean becoming a dilettante at the expense of expertise.

Do you feel as strongly that designers who want to start their own companies should be able to run the business side of things as effectively as the design side? How important is business education for designers?
Designers should try to run the business side. Some designers may be great at it; some may be terrible. Either way, you'll understand business more by trying, and you'll value and empathize with those who do it well. This is not unlike learning to build. Business acumen is a valuable skill set, and it provides important life lessons.

Do you consider yourself an entrepreneur? Have you always wanted to be in ownership of your work?
I consider myself entrepreneurial—with the spirit or characteristics of an entrepreneur.

You're a big proponent of writing. Do you consider yourself a design writer? How do your writing and design practice influence or benefit one another?
Writing is designing for both reading and comprehension experiences. Good writing is a very important part of good interface design. Sometimes you don't need a visual design change; you need a language change.

Writing is also a powerful part of articulating your thinking and sharing it with others. I suppose I'm a 'design writer' in the cases that I've written about design, but more so I'm a designer who writes.

There are many products and sites that build new communities online—Etsy for the marketplace, dribbble for the design process, Medium for writing—what has caused the shift from the individual to the desire to be connected to others and to be a part of something bigger than yourself?
The desire to connect and be part of experiences that are shared and larger than ourselves is an innate part of being human. These online communities you reference are giving visible form to that. They're creating feature sets and communication tools that capture that desire and help to make it happen. They haven't invented the desire though.

How have you seen Etsy's community grow and its users encourage entrepreneurship among each other?
The single biggest way this happens is through knowledge sharing. This happens in informal ways and formal, structured ways. Informal ways include through private messages on Etsy, forums, threads among people with shared interests, and person-to-person at events and casual meetups.

More structured ways include events, programming and materials we create where we explicitly source expertise and stories within the community, package them up, and share them with a wider audience.

You've taken on many roles—design studio founder, Supercorp cofounder, creative director at Etsy—what do you think it means to be a 'designer' in today's environment?
I like Charles Eames' definition of design: 'A plan for arranging elements in such a way as to best accomplish a particular purpose.' With that definition of design, the role of designer is to create said plans and do said arranging. The designer with an entrepreneurial bent is also likely to define the purpose as well.

Additionally, how have you seen design's role change in the startup world?

Design is now acknowledged as an important part of startups. It's not uncommon to hear that good design is no longer a differentiator but is 'table stakes.' It used to be that if there were two comparable products from a feature standpoint that address the same audience, the better designed one would likely succeed or could at least build its brand position around the fact that it was a well-designed option. Today, the audience expects that a product's design be of a high caliber or the product will simply be ignored. In many cases, design is necessary to even enter the conscious of an audience. This is good for design as a profession from a value standpoint. It also puts the onus on designers to tackle higher order challenges.

Do you think now, more than ever, it's important for the design community to write, share their perspective and engage the larger design community? What are some platforms where this can take place?

I believe it's always important for the design community — or any community — to have a dialogue with itself. It's a great way to have healthy debate. It's happening a little bit on Twitter. Dribbble has created healthy dialogue and sharing around a sliver of the process surrounding visual design details and style. Conversations are happening across platforms, and designers jump between these platforms. Branch offers promise in the area of conversation across many topics.

What excites you most about the future of design and the opportunities available to us in today's technological landscape?

Everything! Design is such an awesome enabling and multiplying force. Good can become great with the help of design. What a wonderful power to possess.

Etsy, iPad Application; Design, Dan Betz

Kate Bingaman-Burt | Illustrator, Educator | Portland, OR

What Did I Buy Today: An Obsessive Consumption Journal, Interior Spread

"What worries me is if I look at a project
and think it is a total success."

Kate Bingaman-Burt

Fail in Good Spirits

Kate Bingaman-Burt is an illustrator and educator at Portland State University. She also is a curator, author and ambassador for indie-craft culture and a champion of entrepreneurialism. Kate started her daily drawing project, Obsessive Consumption, in 2006 and hasn't stopped drawing. What started as a side project led to a book contract, and her illustrations were published in the book, Obsessive Consumption: What Did You Buy Today?

She learned firsthand that working on personal projects helps designers figure out what they want to say. Kate has followed her instincts and challenges her students to push self-initiated work to find their own voices.

Can you give a bit of your background and how you came to illustration? How did Obsessive Consumption start?
Obsessive Consumption was actually illustration free until 2006. I relied more on photography and installation methods for the first few years of Obsessive Consumption, which officially started in 2002. I started making work about the things that we buy because I was sick of having notebooks filled with half-assed ideas about our relationship to objects and no execution follow through. The daily drawing project started after a few years of photo documentation, credit card statement drawing, lots of sewing, lots of talking to strangers, and lots of Internet engagement. I started drawing because I didn't like drawing. Now, six years later, I draw every day and I love it.

How does teaching influence your practice?
Teaching plays a huge role. My students inspire me; they challenge me, and they cause me to rethink ways of making and doing. The problem-solving aspect of it is super rewarding, and I think my ability to improv has skyrocketed because of my daily teaching practice. Students also make me really listen. Being a good listener is such a crucial skill, and I work on being better at this every day. Constantly having to talk and think and explain really helps with your own practice, and having an active practice helps your students. It is a weird Möbius strip.

You are an illustrator, an educator and an ambassador for indie-craft culture. We're interested in the entrepreneurial spirit of designers and illustrators. Do you consider yourself to be an entrepreneur?

I am a huge champion of entrepreneurialism and try to cultivate it in my design students, as well as through class assignments and simple encouragement for their independent ideas. I wish I had more time to execute all of the microbusiness ideas that I have floating in my brain. Seriously, coming up with ideas and products and helping students figure out how to execute them is like a sport to me. I get all competitive and sweaty just thinking about it. I guess to answer your question, yes.

As an educator, do you have a perspective on how design education could better prepare students to push personal projects into the market?

From my experience, working on personal projects helps you figure out what you want to say as a designer. If you have a good handle on what you are trying to say and your personal voice then you can help clients figure out what they want to say and help them define their voice. School can help cultivate experimentation, exploration and also provide a framework — deadlines, goals, community, critique — to help execute these ideas. School also provides a supportive community, where you can fail and flail, and hopefully flourish.

Do you think it is beneficial for an illustrator to have a recognizable style? Is a style beneficial to get work but potentially a hindrance to experimentation?

Speaking from experience, I think it is good to cultivate a style and demonstrate evidence of that style in many formats and situations. Again, I didn't think of myself in the illustration context until I started my daily drawing project. Producing a pile of work in a similar style was

really helpful in attracting other illustration opportunities. However, I think you can produce a pile of work in a variety of styles and succeed in that regard as well. Experimentation is difficult to do if you become really busy executing work in one style because this is what is being requested of you, which is not necessarily a bad problem, but it does hinder exploration…if that is something you are searching for.

Consumption is a theme in much of your work. Do you have thoughts on how we consume content online as designers? Do we look at too much work?

I don't think thoughtfully consuming too much visual work is a bad thing. Where it becomes dangerous is when we consume too much visual work and don't think about the context, don't think about the concept, and don't think about the 'why' of looking. It is also harmful if you are only looking at design and design on the Internet for inspiration. Only looking at design and only looking at the Internet leads to headaches and a general yucky feeling. It also makes you want to brush your teeth, go for a run and take a shower. Or maybe that is just me. I can always tell when my students have been looking at the same websites because their moodboards all look the same. This is a conversation I have all of the time: 'Look outside of design. Look outside of Pinterest! Go get lost somewhere looking at tangible things. Go read a damn book — with words, not pictures.'

You're in your seventh year of Obsessive Consumption — is drawing something every day still fun for you?

In the future, I might not always draw as much as I do now, but I do know I will try to keep going with the daily process of drawing a small window into my life. The rewards are too big for something that is so very simple. I love the paper archive that I have created regarding the last six years of my life. For me, the drawings of purchased goods are just a conduit for memories and experiences, reminders of the bigger stories and emotions that are represented in the lines.

Was it your plan to monetize the drawings and turn them into a book?

My plan wasn't to monetize them or to turn them into a book. Little zines, yes, but a book no. My plan was to figure out how to document my life within the framework of executing a simple task, in a similar way, every day. My plan was to figure out how to feel comfortable with a pen in my hand. My plan was to share these drawings with whoever cared to look. I am amazed at the extra surprises and experiences that have come my way through this project. The people whom I have met and the conversations that I have had are incredible.

What is the biggest risk you've taken in your career?

I'm not sure whether I have taken my biggest risk yet. I have a few things on the back burner that make me nervous—in a good way. I think I should probably pull the lever on those.

What is your favorite failure?

Favorite failure? I've had oh so many failures! This isn't meant as a negative thing, however. I always fail in good spirits. What worries me is if I look at a project and think it is a total success. That is when I will get kicked in the ass. Failure is such a severe word. I consider myself so fortunate to be able to work the way that I work. I work with amazing students. I draw fun stuff for fun people. I talk about zines and then help people make them, and I am able to travel because of these things. I make dumb stuff. I sometimes make smart stuff. I hang out with my husband and my dog and eat hot dogs and chips. I explore, make, share and experiment. I am so very fortunate.

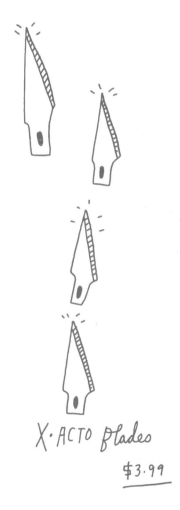

Daily Drawings, X-Acto Blades

Insites: The Book, Interior Spread

"Personal stories resonate with anyone.
 It doesn't matter what you do or who you are."

Elliot Jay Stocks

Create With Passion

Elliot Jay Stocks is a designer, speaker and author. He is one half of Viewport Industries and the founder of typography magazine 8 Faces. *He formed Viewport Industries with his friend, Keir Whitaker, and published* Insites: The Book, *which features a series of interviews with prominent designers in the web community based on an informal Q-and-A tour he led with those in the web and tech communities.*

Elliot's self-initiated publications have built him loyal fans within the design world. His ability to take ideas that he loves and turn them into tangible products has given him the opportunity to pursue a career rooted in his own passions.

Can you tell us a little bit about your background and how you came to design?
Design is the one thing I've done for my entire life. My childhood was spent drawing. My earliest 'client work' was when I was 11 or 12 years old. I designed and illustrated brochures, pamphlets and invitations for events such as school drama productions and parents' evenings. When I was 14, I wrote and illustrated an *X-Men*-esque comic book. I photocopied and sold it to kids at school. I suppose that was the seed that would eventually lead to products such as *8 Faces*. For a long time I was pretty technophobic. My family didn't get a computer until I was 17, which was pretty late considering that was around 1999. The computer we got came with a precursor to Photoshop. I used that program to digitally color a comic book that I put together for an A-level art project.

That was the turning point for me. I took a year off after school before I went to university. During that year, I startled dabbling in web design for my own music projects. I formed a lo-fi record label with friends, and we put out a small-scale release. I did all of the design for the label and the point-of-sale materials. I built a basic website using this basic browser-based WYSIWYG tool, Homestead. I knew that I needed to learn how to do web design properly. I started university and got into Flash, and that was my semiprofessional start in design.

Do you consider yourself an entrepreneur?

I do, and I don't. From the days when I made and sold my own comics, I've always felt that I was an entrepreneur—but I feel like entrepreneurship is a bit of a dirty word. When I think of entrepreneurs, I think of people who aren't involved in the nitty-gritty details of making a product. Those who spend their days in Silicon Valley talking to venture capitalists—that's not me. For me, it's the ownership that's important, not the business side of things.

How important are your side projects to your practice, and what was the catalyst to cofound Viewport Industries?

I've always had side projects, perhaps even to a fault. I suppose it's a symptom of enjoying the kind of work I do. By far my biggest side project is *8 Faces*, and its success was definitely a catalyst. It showed me that you could do something you love and make money from it. The risk is not nearly as big as people make it out to be. Plus, Keir and I were both independently enjoying our respective client projects but didn't feel as motivated as we did when we discussed ideas that we came up with together. The combination of forming our own company with the continuation of profitable side projects meant that there wasn't too much at stake in giving up client work.

How has designing, producing and distributing your own magazine changed the way you think about the rest of your design practice?

8 Faces has probably been the biggest learning experience I've had. Not only because of the content, but also the format. I've learned so much about print design by trying stuff out and seeing what works. I've also taken a lot of that type-centric thinking—baseline grids, optimum measure, etc.—into my web work. From a wider view, *8 Faces* also pushed me to

think more about the big picture of content creation, publishing and transitioning from service to product; *8 Faces* was unlike anything I'd ever done before. I had no idea what I was doing when I started it. I still don't know what I'm doing. There's nothing wrong with making things up as you go.

When you started *8 Faces*, what surprised you about the process?

The actual print design part of it—working in InDesign and laying stuff out—is a relatively small part of the process for me. I hadn't planned on that. Getting sponsorship, chasing invoices, managing assets—that's the stuff that takes all the time, and it came as a massive surprise. That side of things is so demanding that there's no way I would have been able to put out a second issue if the magazine wasn't making money. It's impossible to sustain a project like that when you're only doing it during evenings and weekends.

It's taken me awhile to build a team for *8 Faces* because I find it difficult to let go of control. One of the best choices I ever made was hiring Jon Tan and Stefan Weyer to design the typeface choice spreads. What they create is a thousand times better than what I could do.

What is the most rewarding part of self-publishing?

Seeing people tweet and blog about how much they love the product. It's incredible when they upload photos to Flickr as they unbox it. I think we take the global nature of the web for granted, but it's amazing when a real, physical thing lands on doormats across the world.

People scramble to get *8 Faces* before it sells out. It's immensely rewarding to see that passion—the same passion I have as a creator. I'm always amazed that people feel as enthusiastic about it as they do.

What is the origin of the Insites tour?

Keir and I have a lot of experience on the conference circuit, both as speakers and event organizers. One thing we kept encountering was that the conversation offstage was more interesting than the presentations, at least more relatable in terms of personal stories that others could learn from. That's my motivation for the book, too.

From your experience with *8 Faces* and *Insites: The Book*, what is it about personal stories that resonates with readers?

I think that personal stories resonate with anyone. It doesn't matter what you do or who you are; everyone wants to know how people get from A to B, and 99 percent of the time, that journey consists of small steps, whether you talk to the right person by chance, or put out something that accidentally becomes successful.

Those things lead to bigger things. It's immensely comforting to read others' stories because people see these big names and assume that there's some magical formula that got them to where they are today. But it's actually a series of small steps, just like everyone else. These heroes of the web are humans. Demystifying them always leads to a positive feeling for the reader.

How do your writing and design practice influence or benefit one another? Is writing design and design writing?

I wouldn't say they're the same thing. But I do think it's important that they exist in tandem. It's good to write about design, to document your process, record your mistakes, and help other people who walk similar paths. I love writing. I don't think my design process and my writing process have much in common, but words fascinate me as both a writer and a designer. Not many people can write well, and that's a great shame. If the web were to improve in any way, it would be for everyone to get better at writing.

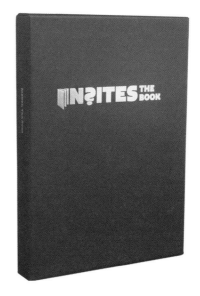

Insites: The Book, Cover

Artwork by Erik Marinovich

This issue's beautiful cover artwork was created by Erik Marinovich, who we first worked with when he designed the third in our series of artwork prints.

On the opposite page, you can see the original artwork behind that print.

8 Faces, Interior Spread

What are your thoughts on the portfolio, and is it important to be known for something?
The only reason I don't have a portfolio on my site is because I still haven't been able to find time to put one together. I'm in a very fortunate position. I'm known for a few projects and lucky that I don't have to have a portfolio online. I'm extremely grateful for that because I don't have time right now to build one. It frustrates me, though. I'm annoyed that I don't have a visual record of my recent projects. That's something all designers should have, regardless of whether you're using a portfolio to get new work.

How does your collaboration with Keir work?
It works well. I'm a designer with some front-end web skills, and he's a developer with some design skills. But it's not merely us meeting in the middle in terms of making websites. We work well together when we discuss business decisions, decide on a creative direction to take, or gather content.

Those scenarios continually prove how well we work together. I think finding someone you gel with is a rare thing. It's not just about skills—it's about the way your minds work together. Keir and I have different tastes, but somehow it really works. We approach things from different angles, yet end up at the same place.

Frank Restaurant, Hand-painted Mural

"I think there has been this turn in the collective
conscious of designers."

Christian Helms

Always Ask for Advice

Christian Helms is a man of many ventures. He's the founder of Helms Workshop, a creative studio, cofounder of Standard Grit, a handmade, limited-edition textile company, and cofounder and designer of Frank, a hotdog and beer joint in Austin, Texas. His work is known for its southern charm, playful, smart wit and classically cool aesthetic.

Christian believes designers have the power to become their own clients, that they can take risks and succeed. He took a risk with Frank—he started a restaurant with zero restaurant experience—and it has become loved not only for the food, but also for the culture and the community it has built. Success defined.

You have a nice balance of client work and self-initiated projects. What are your thoughts on the industry's shift from client services to entrepreneurial ventures?

I think it's a great thing, and I'm excited to see more and more of it. I like to keep at least one self-started venture in the office every year. It can be small, like Standard Grit, or it can be big, like Frank.

If you look at the design industry in the U.S., it is really young in terms of the evolution of a true industry. Nobody's been doing this for very long; Paul Rand was around a week ago, in terms of the long-term evolution of an industry. We've pretty quickly gone from being super service-oriented, as commercial artists, to a place where we can now leverage the conversation to offer so much more equity to business owners. I think there has been this turn in the collective conscious of designers. We realized that we start these businesses for clients, these businesses go on to be successful, and we think, 'Why aren't we starting these businesses?' We know what we're doing; we would be the clients who really trust ourselves, and let ourselves take these big risks and make real statements versus doing what everyone else already did. I think that's a new unifying theme among designers—whether it's a publication, or a restaurant or an axe company. It's exciting, and I hope there's a lot more of it.

There will be successes and failures, but either way, I think this movement is really valuable.

We're a design studio. We're not a little business incubator, but I have a personal interest in building things outside of the business. I don't like to sit down a whole lot, and I like taking on things that I haven't done before.

Frank began as a conversation. My former partner from the Decoder Ring, Geoff, and I loved this hot dog restaurant in Chicago, and we asked ourselves why there wasn't anything like it in Austin. We had to keep going to Chicago to find great hot dogs, and that just didn't seem right—like that's a hell of a commute. Geoff, who is just boundlessly optimistic said, 'Well, we should just start one in Austin.' I said, 'Well you don't know anything about starting a restaurant, and I don't have time.' I like to line up all the reasons you shouldn't do something first and then check them off slowly and break down that wall. Geoff is the opposite. I could call Geoff in five minutes and say, 'We're starting a shoe store in Waco,' and he would be like, 'Fuck yeah we are; let's go!' It's a nice balance between the two of us, where I'm like, 'Slow the fuck down!,' and he's like, 'Let's run real fast at the wall.'

We talked about Frank a lot, and we knew that there was a definite hole in the market here. No one was doing anything like this. About the same time we both started hanging around Woodland, a restaurant in South Austin. We met Daniel Northcutt, who did operations and management there—and for the restaurant that used to be here before Frank, and it was a perfect storm.

The three of us were sitting around the table drinking beer, and we realized that we had everything we needed in terms of ability to start a restaurant. We brought my younger brother, who's a chef, down from North Carolina to serve as the executive chef for the first year to set up the menu. The whole restaurant was a very bootstrap effort. The mural was painted by Daniel, the manager, my brother, Matt, and Geoff's wife.

We were going to hire a sign painter, but they thought they could save money—and I didn't think they could paint—so they waited until I went to North Carolina and painted it while I was gone. They did a great job—and anything that they didn't do a good job with, I took a hammer and hit so it's 'antiqued' in the areas that didn't look right. So much of that restaurant was built in a similar manner with lots of DIY solutions.

We took over a giant building and did work that required some capital, but it was very 'car tires and chicken wire' in the beginning in terms of putting in sweat equity and building it ourselves. I like to say, I don't know anything about running a restaurant, and in the day-to-day I don't, but in terms of building something, we were all really committed.

What was the time frame from the idea to the time it opened?
Less than a year. God, it's such a blur. We talked about it, and then all of the sudden we had investors and a space. Once that moment hit, it was like, 'Yeah, it's time to go.' The economy crashed in the middle of the renovation, so we lost two-thirds of our promised investors in the beginning. We just said, 'Screw it,' opened with a third of our investment, put in more sweat equity, and it completely worked. The response to the restaurant was immediate. It took off really quickly, and the response has grown so steadily. It's been a great partnership between three very different people who offer three very different things. We all do our best at respecting the other's expertise and viewpoint, and it works well.

To start something such as Frank, is it important to have varied skill sets on board?
It's really important at the beginning to sit down and look at what you're good at and be

honest with yourself about what you're not good at and what you don't know how to do. There's enough of a hump to get over in terms of continued learning in day-to-day design. If you try to teach yourself to run a gigantic restaurant while you're doing it — and you've never been part of that industry — it's like designing your own logo if you've never designed a logo, probably not a good idea. You need to recognize the areas that you need help in, and get partners who can help you.

Also, ask for advice from everybody. I'm a huge fan of asking for help. When I started my own studio, and even as a young designer, I would talk to more experienced people like James Victore, Art Chantry, John Bielenberg

Frank Restaurant, Logo

and Michael Bierut, and I would ask them questions constantly. People love to talk about themselves, so it's not hard to get answers, especially if you buy them a beer. You can learn a lot, as long as you don't drink too much beer during those meetings. It's helpful to actually remember what was said.

We've found that people are willing to talk to us, too, and share their stories.
It's a cool community. I get requests like yours all the time, but I can kind of tell the people who have their shit together, with a cool idea that they're committed to, who aren't just a couple of stoned design kids who are like, 'I want to hang out with that dude.'

Did you always know that you wanted to open a restaurant? Or is Frank more about the opportunity that you identified?
No! If you told me when I went to college that I would end up in Texas and that I would open a restaurant, I would have been like, 'What the fuck went wrong? That's terrible!' But it's been an amazing experience. So that proves for the 50th time that I wasn't that bright when I went off to college.

We're all—my partners hate the term 'foodies' and I'm not supposed to use it—super into food, and we are all geeks. I'm a beer geek; I'm a design geek, and I'm a food geek. We all like weird, unique restaurants that we find when we travel. I'll call Geoff and say, 'I'm in Portland, Maine, and I just had a lobster roll next to a group of three-legged dog enthusiasts. It's amazing up here!' We're into weird, quirky culture.

We looked at cities around the country, and the hot dog thing was getting interesting, but no one had done it here. We did identify a hole in the market. It wasn't a situation where we said, 'We want to start a restaurant. What should it be?' We've since talked to a lot of folks who want to put a Frank in other cities. They are the kind of people who say, 'I really want to start a

Frank Restaurant, Wooden Nickel

restaurant. What should it be?' We generally say no. We built a really articulated brand here. It's not subtle, and you can't plug it into a mini mall. Franchises may happen eventually, but we'll start with partners.

It also would lose the authenticity and the special factors associated with this one.

The restaurant embodies everything that we seem to love. It's weird in all the right ways, and you can't hand it off to someone else to do it the way you want it to be done.

What was the design path that led up to you landing in Texas?

I went to Portfolio Center in Atlanta, and I managed to win an internship with Michael Bierut. That was huge. I was fortunate enough to get to work on projects that interns don't normally get to do. I got to work on projects that were just mine and Michael's. It was phenomenal. After I finished school, Hank Richardson, director of design at Portfolio Center, told me, 'You gotta go back to New York. You know everybody there; you know people who folks don't know 15 or 20 years in, and you should go.' New York was not the right fit for me, and I knew it, but I went anyway. I took a job that was the wrong fit and lived in a city that was the wrong fit. I was like, 'Fuck, what have I done? I've royally fucked up here.' There was also this naïve belief that your first job out of school really defines your career. I didn't know what I was doing. I paid for grad school on my own dime, and I thought, 'I'm in trouble.'

John Bielenberg had just started Project M, and I was so jealous of the people involved with it. I decided that I had to be a part of it. It would be a way for me to jump off a bad job and do something of value rather than just quit my first job after a month. I put all my student loans into forbearance, I called John and said, 'I want to be part of Project M.' I met Art Chantry, one of the advisers there, and we became buddies. I really had a meltdown, one of those ridiculous quarter-life crises. I didn't know what I was doing anymore; I didn't want to be in New York. I thought I was throwing my career away. If that was all true, I at least wanted to live somewhere that I liked. I had visited Austin with James Victore. I thought, 'The city is great. They have old neon signs, good food, cheap beer, a trail by the lake...why don't I go live there?' I decided that if I could just get there and get some kind of design job, I'd be happy. I got here, and I got a design job, but after six months I was like, 'Ok, what am I really gonna do?' It just kind of went from there. That's how I ended up in Austin. I moved here because I loved the city.

Once I got here, I tried to meet everybody who was doing something interesting—not just designers either. I met photographers; I met chefs; I met sign makers, such as Todd Sanders, who creates vintage-inspired neon signs; I met writers. I met anybody who was doing something awesome, and I would just buy 'em a beer. They were all doing amazing work that I could clearly tell they loved, and I loved what I was doing, so I just wanted to talk to them and share what I was doing, too.

Is Austin a pretty tight-knit community?

It is. It's grown a lot, but when I first got here it seemed like there were just seven design dudes. It was like these are the guys to know. You would just kind of find them, and then it haloed out from there. Now it's bigger.

There are folks like DJ Stout who have been around for a while and then folks like me who have been around for a little while, and folks like the Public School guys who are finding their feet and figuring out their own path. It's nice because everybody kind of looks at each other and nods and throws work back and forth to each other. It's small enough that everybody knows each other and pays attention to each other in a way that fosters healthy competition.

Your undergrad degree was in journalism. Is writing part of your practice? How did you move from journalism to design?

I grew up in a little town in North Carolina, and I didn't know you could do design for a living. The only design I saw as a kid was on things such as Doritos bags, and I never thought that people made those things. I thought they just came out of a machine or something. In terms of signage around the town, it was like a hillbilly scrawled it on a piece of wood. Those were my two references, and there wasn't much overlap in between, so I just went to college and focused on what I was good at within my narrow scope of understanding.

University of North Carolina was the best school that I got into, and I was really excited. I did creative writing in high school, and I was offered some writing scholarships, and I decided, 'Well, I guess I'm a writer.' I went to journalism school and took journalism classes mixed with a few really bad studio art classes, and I started to try to put them together. I said, 'Oh, I'll do a painting, and I'll do a writing piece for it,' and it was just clunky and weird. I still have really bad paintings in a box in the garage. I don't think I can throw them away, but I'm sure as hell not going to take them out of the box.

Toward the end of college, I took an intro to design class, and I was like, 'This is it; this is the whole thing.' I found it and then I realized I wasn't good at it, so I went to Portfolio Center.

Writing is engrained in me and is a big part of what I do at the studio. Writing and design are just one and the same to me. It's storytelling. I write for clients. Once I get a sense of the core personality of the brand, the copywriting blossoms out from there.

You use writing as a tool to identify a brand's direction?

Absolutely. It's where I start to articulate the heart and purpose of a brand. It is also a driver of content for murals, signs, typography and everything that follows. There's an editorial viewpoint and voice to every brand we work on.

As far as personal fulfillment, how does a project such as Frank compare to a client project, in which you get to create something really awesome for them?

The official answer is I am equally fulfilled by client projects as I am by my own projects. The unofficial answer is how can you not be more fulfilled by something like Frank, that's yours? That said, I have clients like Austin Beerworks that I am equally proud of. I'm so happy with what we've built together, and how we're growing and evolving as collaborators.

Because you're as much a part of that?

Yeah, I love those guys; they are a phenomenal client in that they trusted me. They sat down, and they believed what I told them to be true, and took a risk based on the idea that they should be different in a crowded marketplace. And it's been a really successful experience for them. They made an impact immediately within the industry.

You've been with them from the beginning?

They didn't even have a name when I first started meeting with them. I worked with them on a temporary name for business cards that they could hand to potential investors, I worked with them on branding, identity, packaging, web design, everything. I work with them constantly to continue to grow the brand.

Now that you've built tangible brands, do you find that it's easier to get client work?

Frank and Austin Beerworks are great teaching tools for other clients to see what we're all about. I use Austin Beerworks in new client meetings all the time because they'll say, 'Oh, I love it so much.' Then I say, 'You might not have loved it if you were the client.' I wouldn't let the brand look like traditional craft beer.

Standard Grit, Handmade Textiles

In the beginning I said, 'Let's make a list of what beer looks like.' They said, 'Hops, streams, mountains, cascading streams, fields, bicycles, you know all the things that beer looks like.' I said, 'Nope, nope, nope and nope. We have to talk about what you're really about, and we have to articulate that through design.' Then we crafted something that doesn't look like other beers. That move has been hugely successful for them, but for most clients, that's terrifying. Because they don't look like a brand that says 'beer,' then they have to stand on their own two feet and defend it. They have to take a stand. That scares the hell out of a lot of people, so I love using that example in new client meetings. I bring it back up when clients try to deviate away from the idea. I say, 'Well, why don't you just look like Joe's Crab Shack then? Why don't you just walk and talk like every other brand out there? You'll blend in seamlessly.'

Is most of your work branding?

We keep a pretty diverse range of stuff in the studio. At any given time, there are a couple of big brand projects. Then there are a couple of music projects and a lot of packaging design. We just did a custom packaging project for the Alamo Drafthouse. We came up with the idea to design and brand a wine each year based on a different movie. The first film we partnered with was *The Princess Bride*. It was so much fun, and I'm hugely proud of that, too.

When you leave design school, you have your portfolio, and you're sitting there thinking you'll never get to design wine packaging, and you'll definitely never get to design wine packaging based on one of your favorite movies. No one gets that, but we did!

We got to work with the Alamo Drafthouse and design something for one of our favorite movies. That's pretty unbelievable. Inconceivable!

Frank Restaurant, Business Card

We want to champion the notion that designers can do everything they want and more. There's no reason to believe they cant. That's part of the reason why I love what you guys are doing. The more you do what you love, the more people stop trying to stop you from doing it. Once you've done it a couple of times, people start to notice, and they start to come to you just for that work. Then you'll find yourself saying, 'Really, you're in?'

Your 20s are the time to be reckless and bold and poor, and to seriously work your hardest to build something that you care about. Then you monetize that in your 30s. You can probably skew that a little younger today. I was just a late bloomer. That first part of your career, you just have to work your ass off to make those things happen that you want to be exemplary for what you want to do next. Don't just tiptoe in, play it safe and follow the rules — you can follow the rules later. Once you have a house, a wife and a kid, sure, follow the rules. Or don't! But when you're young, and just barely making rent, break as many rules as you can to push toward that thing you want to do. No one's going to offer you your dream job.

Do you have a structure at the studio to work on self-initiated ideas? Up until this point, the entrepreneurial stuff has been generated by me and generally only worked on by me. I don't often use studio resources for that — but that model is going to shift in the coming years. I encourage everyone to work on freelance, which is kind of rare. I like a lot of projects going on in the studio, and I think it's important, especially for our younger, greener designers. I encourage everyone to take on freelance outside of our work because I think it helps them learn. As a young designer, experience is good, and experience with stuff going wrong is even better.

Culturally, we are a very laid-back studio, but we're laid back because everybody really takes care of their shit, and I trust them, so I don't have to be a micromanager. Or I should say I'm learning to give them space to make the work their own. It's hard. But they make us look good, and that's good for everybody.

You've said that you don't like giving advice. I've talked about the whole 'famous designer' thing, and I have plenty of friends who might fall into that category, but I'm just not comfortable with it for me, not that I even qualify, necessarily. I'm just not comfortable giving out big, bold brash advice and saying, 'Design should be this or design should be that.' It's much more personal, organic and situational.

You have been selective about interviews and don't prescribe to the networking thing. I've been a big fan of just putting my head down and doing the work. I think it's probably a little bit of naïveté, too. I just assumed if the work was great, people would notice, and it's so not true. But I also think that same philosophy let us build a studio and a nice body of work without being 'out there' as much, which is nice. I'm also just not good at it. In recent years I've worried that it might paint me as snobbish, but the truth is I'm an introvert by nature. I like to focus on the work. I focus on business development because it brings in the work and after that, the cheerleading part. There's only so much time in the day, and I'd rather be doing the work, or bringing in the work, than doing the, "the 'hey, hey, look at me' part." There's a pretty good history in our industry of people who sell better than they design. It would just break my heart to be that dude. I would rather be sold less and have a little bit more craft in our work. I really think that's a predominate theme in what I'm seeing these days — craft. At the end of the day, the proof is in the pudding, and I'd rather be recognized for the work that we do than the way we sold some slick thing. It's just not my thing or my skill set.

Have you gained any insight from working with partners?

I ran a collective studio for a little bit; we had three partners, and none of us were that experienced at the time. We've all grown a lot since then. Partnerships are hard. They're great, but they can be terrible in other ways. Decoder Ring started as a little collective making band posters. I dragged it toward a brand direction; we all dragged it in different directions, and at the end of the day, we realized that we all wanted to work on different stuff. We wrung the Decoder sponge as much as we could.

It's just one of those things that ran its course. It was a great start for sure. Running a studio, outside of that, is work. It's the part of the job that's not the sexy design part, but it's really fulfilling when it hits on all cylinders.

For a graphic designer who wants to be and do so many things, the 'T-shaped person' no longer seems to fit. What are your thoughts?

I built myself into a semi-T-shaped person just by virtue of my journalism background and the need to learn about so many different things, including design. But I'm not into the idea that you need to be a certain-shaped person or a 'so-and-so' brand; it should just be whatever works best for you.

Hot dogs. Beer. Rock and roll. Those are things that we all love. That's why we work on them. I don't know what shape that would be — I'll go with hot dog-shaped person.

When you started Frank, did you think you had to know everything there is to know about running a restaurant?

I knew I would manage the brand development and a lot of the environment build-out. We had to have somebody involved who knew restaurant management. There is no way I would have tried to do it all. I also gotta run a design studio and spend time with my family.

You've talked about the importance of craft. How does it inform your practice?

I started Standard Grit partly because I missed handwork. So much of the work we do starts by hand and evolves from there.

Some of my favorite work is the nondesign work. My wife and I renovated our house over the past three years together, and it just frees your mind up. I've come up with so many design solutions while I was sanding something or doing some ridiculous thing in the yard. It's good for us just as humans to create with our hands. There's a satisfaction in doing it. As a student, all I did was live in the sketchbook. As you evolve and start to run a business, you get further away from using your hands, so I'm trying to make an effort to get back to it.

I think people react differently to work crafted by the human hand. It's like the Doritos bag I mentioned earlier. You think, 'Is this made by people?' There is a disconnect from humanity. People treat handcrafted work with a different reverence and connect to it in a different way. Even if you're just like my parents, and you don't know why you like it more, you consider it in a different way. It feels true.

Did growing up in the South influence your move to Austin and support your desire to make things by hand?

Growing up in the South definitely influenced my move to Austin. I think if I could live anywhere, I might live in the mountains of North Carolina. But I would just be designing for the squirrels; I couldn't do what we do there. Austin felt like a happy medium between something that had some momentum but was still growing as a city. The southern thing is weird. When I was growing up, I couldn't wait to get out of there. I was like, 'It's redneck, and it's racist.' I saw all of the negative sides because as a kid you just want to flee. As you grow up, you learn to appreciate your roots. I love the South, and I love the area that I grew up in.

I spoke in San Francisco and someone said, 'If I had to pick a word to describe your work it would be 'southern.' What do you think about that?' I was like, 'Fuck, I've never thought about that, and I don't even know if it's true, but I love that you said that.' It made me tear up, and it's always stuck with me. It makes me really happy because the South has such a cool aesthetic, heritage and history that I'm really proud of. Not the whole slavery thing, not so proud of that. Or Paula Deen.

But in the South there is a consideration for the small things. Like the way you make food, the way you take care of your home, and the way you give a kid a pocketknife because he will own that pocketknife until he's an adult.

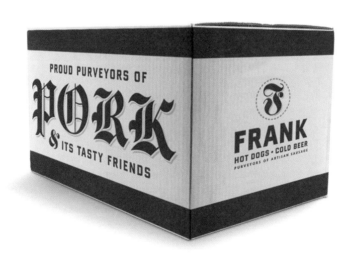

Frank Restaurant, Packaging

I really appreciate the little things. If any of that shows in my work, it's definitely not conscious, but that would be pretty cool.

What are your thoughts on the portfolio? Polished, final work versus process? Is the portfolio even relevant in the age of social media and building a reputation online?

I mean, the short answer is I have no idea how important a portfolio is in that regard. But I will say I would be much more excited about a piece of work that tells a story and takes me through an experience than something that just looks really hot. People can make beautiful work, but if it doesn't serve a purpose or create a story to experience, then it just looks cool.

People with a cultural sensitivity who create great experiences and tell great stories, they will always rise to the top.

Do you think you have an identifying style, and if so, is it a challenge to change it?

Probably at times, but it's something that I work really hard to break out of. When you've done something so many times, you can grab the TV remote in the dark, turn it on and find the channel you want. You don't even have to look at the remote because you've done that muscle move so many times. Design is the same way, and that scares the shit out of me. I have watched folks who have been 'the guy,' and then all of a sudden, that style is out, so they're out. Trends will always ebb and flow, so it's important to have an editorial viewpoint in the way you design and an angle that is uniquely yours. An aesthetic serves that, but it's about having a viewpoint.

I've started to make a list of five things that I can't do on a project, and it puts me back in a design school mind-set. I have to find my feet again, and it sucks.

I'm 35. I'm at the point where designers are supposed to start to suck. Theoretically, your best ideas are supposed to happen before you're

32. You get complacent and repetitive after the age of 32. I'm like, 'Fuck; I don't want to do that.'

Is it important for designers to share their perspective to further the field? Do you speak often?

I used to. I've dialed it back recently because I've made the transition from the young guy who's really excited to the guy who's getting slightly older and realizes he doesn't know everything. Not that I thought I knew everything before, but I just don't want to tell people what they should do. I'm also uncomfortable standing up and showing my work and saying it's important. It's all important, and it's all an evolution. When I was young, I thought, 'I'm young; I'm fiery; I want to do great work, and I'm trying real hard.' It was an underdog thing. Now, as my wife has pointed out to me many times, I can't be the underdog anymore. She says, 'You run a studio; you work on substantial projects; you can't be that guy anymore. You can't do talks like that anymore.' If I do talks again, I have to figure out what I would say. And it shouldn't be, 'Hooray me!'

What do you want the theme of your career to be?

If I knew it would be for me. It's not a teaching tool; it's the way I want to live my life.

We think that growth has a lot to do with the transparency of everyone's work and an acceptance of collaboration. People are starting to realize it's in their best interest to join up with their friends and peers.

Over the past 10 to 15 years, the design industry has worked really hard to legitimize itself to some degree. We can now leverage design as a viable asset to big businesses, so that we can charge huge amounts for it. It's good for everyone's pocketbooks and the industry. But it's also really dulled the conversation from talking about how fun this shit is. It's nice to hear, 'Yes it's good for business, but we also love doing it.' The creative aspect is exhilarating and frustrating, but if it works well it's huge. I recently made the biggest presentation of my career, and we were up against huge, established studios. Instead of just talking about brand equity and business, I talked about the value and payoff of having fun in creating something. And to my surprise and delight, it really resonated and set us apart.

Amid all of the fun, do we need to be critical? Is design criticism necessary?

If people would spend less time criticizing design and more time practicing their craft, we would be in a much better place as a profession. I've never taken part in it because to me it should just be about doing the work. I've been lucky enough to know a few people in my life who have the wherewithal to just do great work, not talk about it, and just let it be. That's been an important reminder for me. Design criticism is important; critical analysis of anything is good, but it can be more of a conversation.

The design industry seems to be moving away from the revered 'rock-star designer' toward a community mind-set.

Technology is a huge part of that. There is just so much prevalent work online these days. The *Communication Arts Annual* came out once a year, and you would see a guy who had like 17 things in there, and then he was 'the guy.' He was the guy who was speaking; he was the guy who got featured, and now stuff is so much more fluid that it just goes everywhere. It's such a small, weird, insular world. Being a famous designer is like being a famous plumber. It's like all the other plumbers are like, 'He plumbs like a motherfucker.'

Any last advice for designers who want to pursue entrepreneurial ventures?

Be 100 percent yourself. If you do that, and if you work on stuff that you love and care about, then you can create a community. An extended community of people who either love that same stuff, or love what they do with just as much fire. And there's a parallel there, regardless of industry. I've found writers, musicians and other creatives all over town and the country who make work that either locks up really well with what we do or is completely different— but it works toward common goals. It's such an amazing community to be a part of, and I feel really fortunate that we've been able to grow that. That's exactly what you guys are furthering with what you're building. Congratulations.

Frank Restaurant, Signage

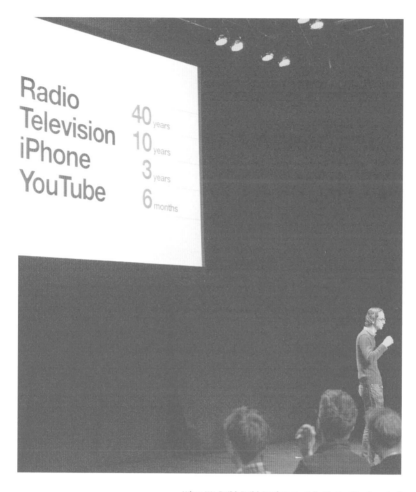

When We Build, Build Conference Talk; Photo, Filly Campbell

"To design anything useful, you need to
understand how the world works."

Wilson Miner

Be Curious,
and Ask Questions

Wilson Miner believes that we have the power and the tools to change the world. He believes that design comprises the choices we make about the world we want to live in, and that we make our world what it is and in turn become the kind of people who live in it. Wilson crafted web experiences as interactive designer for Apple and as the head of design at Rdio, a digital music service. He currently works as a digital product designer at Facebook.

Wilson's work has helped highlight the importance of a product's design — whether the product is a web framework or social network. He understands that we need to think broadly about the world, what we build, and how we learn the skills we need to create meaningful work.

Can you give us a little bit about your background and how you came to design?

I've been playing around on computers since I was old enough to use one. My dad used to get these educational kids' games for the Apple II, so I say I learned to read from computer games. When I was about 10 years old, my dad got me a game called Cosmic Osmo — a kids' game made by Cyan, the people who went on to make Myst. It was made with HyperCard, this amazing software for the Mac that was kind of a precursor to the web. Everything was based on a metaphor of a stack of 'cards,' and you could build all kinds of things — from databases to games — by linking the cards together and scripting all kinds of actions. My dad bought a copy of HyperCard, and I spent hours making half-finished adventure games with terrible jokes and really bad art. But I think that's really what got me started in what we think of now as interaction design.

Do you consider yourself an entrepreneur? Have you always wanted to be in ownership of your work?

I don't think I have the entrepreneurship gene. I'm not good at pitching things, and I'm not fueled by the excitement of risk the way some people are — it just feeds into my anxiety and makes it hard for me to focus on what I do enjoy, which is working on a product.

Independence and ownership are great, but there's a lot of energy that goes into other things when you're out there on your own.

How important is writing to your practice?
I've actually kind of given up on writing, at least publicly on a blog. I started a blog as an excuse to have a site of my own to play with new designs outside of client work. The writing was just something to do to fill it in with content. Writing is a great discipline, and over the years I've written one or two things I'm still proud of, but it's just not something I gravitate to as much anymore, at least in that format.

Do you think now more than ever, it's important for the design community to write, share their perspectives and engage the larger design community?
I do. I think sharing ideas and an articulate debate is always important but especially in times of change. There are some great voices emerging in the design community and some great new outlets for them, such as *The Manual*, *Contents* magazine or *Offscreen* magazine. These are carefully crafted collections with a distinct editorial perspective and a real attention to refining the content — they don't just churn out posts and click 'publish.'

You've spent a lot of time crafting new platforms, and you've redesigned existing platforms. We're interested in new platforms for the design community to share meaningful dialogue, share their perspectives and engage the design community. What are your thoughts on what some of these platforms could be?
I love that we're writing and publishing physical magazines and journals about digital design. Kickstarter has been a huge part of that, and I think it's also been an interesting platform itself for design 'dialogue' in the form of building actual physical products and putting

them out into the world. That's a really articulate way to share a perspective on design: Make something. Kickstarter creates an opportunity for new voices to participate in that kind of exchange of ideas by enabling people to create and share something they couldn't have otherwise and also lets a whole community of people participate in the process who all really want to see that thing exist.

How have you seen design's role change in the startup world over the years?
We've definitely crossed over a threshold in the startup world, where it's an assumption that it's a good idea to pay attention to design from the very beginning. But there's still a big gap in understanding what that means and how to find designers who can contribute in a meaningful way to the early stages of product design. We have a responsibility as designers to step up to the plate here. We're invited to the table now — we need to bring something to it.

Do you think the design of a product, tool or app should be integrated from day one?
Everything that happens in the early days of forming a product is design. You make choices about what a product is, how it will work and its architecture. These decisions will fundamentally shape the product. This isn't the sacred realm of people with 'design' in their job title — a lot of the most important design decisions happen in code — but I do think it helps to have a designer's perspective as part of the conversation from the beginning.

Do you think it's necessary for designers to be educated in business? Or is this something that can be learned as you go?
To design anything useful, you need to understand how the world works. That is not limited to business. You need to be curious; you need to be observant, and you need to ask questions — about everything.

What excites you most about the future of design and the opportunities available to us in today's technological landscape?

So many things are possible today that weren't possible just two years ago—not just on the web. Screens are everywhere, and we can do so much with them, and our opportunity to have an impact is multiplying very quickly. I think about the industrial-design renaissance around the middle of the 20th century—the Eames, Dieter Rams—and I really think we're at a point where we're seeing a changing of the guard. The physical products are still really important, but in a lot of places, they're receding into the background as the screen comes to the forefront.

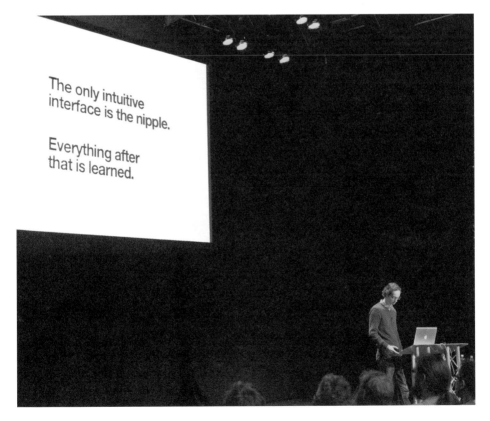

When We Build, Build Conference Talk; Photo, Filly Campbell

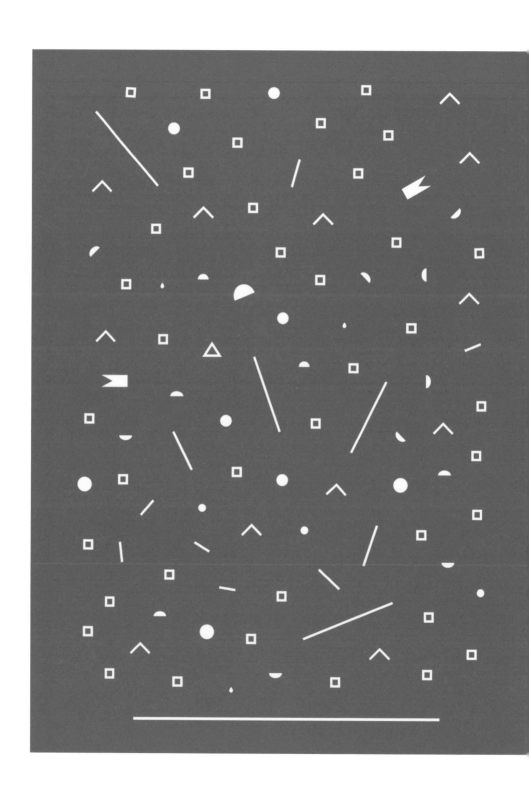

Dan Provost | Cofounder, Studio Neat | Brooklyn, NY

Glif, Tripod Mount and Stand for iPhone

"As a general rule, we like to solve problems
  that we ourselves have."

Dan Provost

Give It a Go

Dan Provost and Tom Gerhardt are two designers who enjoy making simple things and making things simple. They founded Studio Neat with two minimal products — the Glif, a tripod mount and stand made for the iPhone, and the Cosmonaut, a wide-grip stylus for touchscreens — both of which are fully crowdfunded products made possible by Kickstarter and a community of people who believed in their idea.

They wanted to make a physical product but weren't a large company with access to resources; however, they knew there was another way. Studio Neat proves that what once might have taken a team of designers, investors, administrators and logistics people is now possible through crowdfunding, hard work and a few online tools.

Can you tell us about your background and Tom's? Do you have any advice for someone trained in graphic design who wants to make a physical product?

Tom and I both received our undergraduate degrees as Bachelors of Environment Design, which is in the school of architecture at Texas A&M. It was a pretty open-ended design program, as neither of us were interested in pursuing straight-up architecture.

After graduating in 2007, we both moved to NYC to attend grad school. I went to Parsons, earning an MFA in Design and Technology, and Tom attended NYU, and completed the Tisch Interactive Telecommunications Program.

In terms of advice, this quote from Stanley Kubrick has always stuck with me: 'Perhaps it sounds ridiculous, but the best thing that young filmmakers should do is get hold of a camera and some film and make a movie of any kind at all.' I think this applies to everything. The best way to learn is to just jump in and try to do it.

Were you working as designers at the time you decided to develop the Glif? Did the project evolve in the evenings while you were working a full-time job, or did you fully dedicate your time to its development?

Yes, Tom and I were both working full time when we developed the Glif. At the time, Tom and his wife lived in the same apartment complex as me and my wife, only four floors above us, so it was quite convenient to work on it in the evenings and weekends.

Do either of you have a background in business? If yes, how did this aid you in launching Glif? If not, are there any resources you utilized and could suggest to others?
No business background. The only resource that comes to mind is *Rework*, by Jason Fried and David Heinemeier Hansson. Most of our 'business' decisions rely mostly on our intuition and what we deem to be honest and fair. We're flying by the seat of our pants a little bit, but this ties back into the Kubrick quote. Perhaps the best way to learn about business is to start one.

How did you get the idea for the Glif? Were you solving a problem that you faced in your own iPhone experience as a user?
Exactly. I had just got the iPhone 4 in June of 2010 and was blown away by the quality of the camera. I was shooting some video with it and realized how nice it would be to mount it to a tripod. I shared the idea with Tom, and we were both excited about it. As a general rule, we like to solve problems that we ourselves have.

You've said Parson's 'Internet Famous' class helped you understand what makes the web tick. You advised those looking to promote a project to seek out an influential blogger within their product's niche. Do you have any other advice concerning the way you think the Internet works?
I think it's really important to be tapped into your niche. Subscribe to RSS feeds, follow people on Twitter who are doing interesting things, listen to podcasts, etc. I shouldn't have to say that; if you are super excited and obsessed with something, you will already be doing that. Anyhow, over time you will begin to notice a certain cadence and rhythm to all of the noise, and it will become possible to insert yourself

into the conversation. Hopefully that's not too abstract. Long story short, follow things on the Internet that you think are interesting.

You reached your Kickstarter goal the first day you launched the Glif campaign. Would you change anything about your Kickstarter campaign now that you can look back upon its success?
I'm not sure whether we would change anything. I would be interested to know whether the Cosmonaut campaign would have had the same success without doing the 'pay-what-you-want' experiment.

Kickstarter helped limit the financial risk associated with launching your project. What were some of the other risks you had to overcome during the process?
This biggest thing to overcome was probably just our lack of knowledge about manufacturing. We had a lot of learning to do in a short period of time, and even finding a manufacturer was a bit of a shot in the dark. We were very fortunate to get hooked up with vendors who were able to work with us, an unusual client for them.

Can you describe the collaboration between you and Tom on the Glif and Cosmonaut? Do your skill sets overlap, or did you decide to collaborate because you are both good at different things?
We decided to collaborate simply because we are good friends, and have similar tastes and design sensibilities. But, fortunately, our skills complement each other quite well. Crudely defined, I'm more 'front-end,' and Tom is more 'back-end,' but there is a lot of pitching in and both of us just doing what needs to be done.

How do you think your knowledge of the design process translated into the ability to create a business?
I think the skills of a designer can honestly be

translated to anything—because it all boils down to problem solving.

You released *It Will Be Exhilarating*, a book that shares what you've learned from two successful Kickstarter projects. Why a book, and what did you learn from the process?
A couple months after shipping the Glif, I wrote up a post mortem on my blog, outlining all of the things we learned along the way in designing and launching our first physical product. A lot of folks told us this blog post was extremely helpful, so we thought we could perhaps expand it into a full-length book, seeing as we had released two additional products and learned many more things since the blog post was first written. We wrote the book to give encouragement and advice to others seeking to chart a path similar to ours, but we also thought it would be a fun challenge and a bit of a departure from our previous products. I find writing to be mostly torturous, but it is a great way to organize thoughts and ideas, and is an exercise in learning how to effectively communicate.

Do you have any additional advice for a designer, working in a traditional role for clients, who has the desire to turn a personal idea into a viable business?
My advice is do it. You don't have to go 'all in' initially; start small. Tom and I brought the Glif to market while still maintaining our full-time jobs. There are so many great and cheap tools for making great stuff; there are very few excuses to not at least give it a go.

Cosmonaut, Wide-Grip Stylus for Touch Screens

Andy McMillan | Founder, Fiction | Belfast, Northern Ireland

The Manual, Issue One

"The people in the web community, more than any other community I've ever been able to be involved with, are so nice."

Andy McMillan

Build a Community

Andy McMillan builds communities and creates new platforms for design discourse — he does this in person and in print. He started a new kind of design conference with Build, a weeklong festival in Belfast, and The Manual, *a book series that archives meaningful conversation about the web profession and explores who we are as designers.*

Both Build and The Manual *move beyond the personal blog, the individual author and the singular perspective. They represent today's designers as a group, and as a movement. Andy captures the voices of our profession and brings clarity to the "why of web design."*

Can you tell us a bit about how you first got interested in design?
I've been designing websites since I was a kid — which is basically how everyone gets into it — I just fooled around on my computer in the evenings. I've done that for as long as I can remember. I never really took it seriously, and I never thought I could do it as a career, so I went to Queens University in Belfast and studied music technology. After two years, I realized I despised it. I originally wanted to get into producing video documentaries for the BBC. That was my dream job. I wanted to become director general for the BBC.

Web design was just something I did in the evening. I would leave classes that I despised and unwind by working on the web. I taught myself HTML, CSS and JavaScript by building sites for my friends. I felt like I could do something and achieve something. After about two years, I said, 'I can't stand this course anymore. I'm going to take a chance and do the only other thing I know how to do, which is build websites.' I dropped out of the course and started freelancing. Everyone goes through a time when he or she takes a crummy job to get by, and for a while, that's what I did. It was just fun to design as 'a job.' I got bigger and better clients, and it started to look like design could be an actual career. I did that for three or four years. At the same time, I jumped into the web design community and met local people. I also ran meetups and went to conferences, and I quickly realized their weak points. The events that attracted large numbers often turned commercial in order to support the team required to run them. The more popular the events got, the more people they needed to run them, and, the more people they needed to run them, the more money they had to bring in to support the staff. The events started to become less about the talks and more about getting as many sponsors as possible.

I remember sitting in London with friends, ranting about rubbish events, and someone turned around and said, 'If you're going to sit around and complain about these things all the time, then you should just shut up and do your own.' A month and a half later, I booked the venue, came up with a name and contacted speakers. I had no idea what I was doing. I had run local meetups for a while, and I didn't think it would be much harder than that. I thought I might be able to make some money out of it. Obviously, it didn't quite turn out that way. It's a lot more work than the 20-year-old version of me thought it would be. Certainly, there's much less money in it than I thought there would be.

The first Build conference went really well and gained a great reputation. It took off because it was small and really manageable. I was able to spend a lot of time with the speakers. I took them to the cinema one evening, and I bought them dinner and drinks, and everyone went back and said, 'This is different because the organizer actually hung out with us.' People came and had a good time, but it was also great that the speakers went home and said, 'This is a good event to be involved in.'

When was the first Build?
It was in 2009, and 2012 was our fourth year.

Has the conference grown?
It really hasn't. It's always been about 300

Build, Logo

people. The only thing that changes is that I add more 'stuff' every year. The first year Build was just the conference. We screened Gary Hustwit's film 'Objectified' the night before the conference, and there was an after party; that was it—it was very small. The 2012 conference included an entire week of programming. There was a full evening of film, workshops, two evening lectures, an open-book exam and a beer festival. We brewed our own IPA. The attendee count has never been more than 300 to 350 people. I didn't scientifically calculate that number; it just seems to fit. When I walk into the conference, I know I can talk to most of the people there. That's nice. As opposed to walking into a room of 1,200, where you stay with your own friends because you know you won't be able to talk to everyone. There's a real sense of community. There is also a good number of people who return to Build every year. They know each other, and they come back. It's on the calendar.

Did you know there was a good group of people in Belfast that wanted something like Build?

There are a couple of answers to that. There's a massive group of web designers in Belfast. There's great energy in the local web community, and it's not just designers; it's everyone involved in the web. Traditional design agencies here don't talk to each other. They're scared to mention what they are working on for fear that someone will steal their jobs. It's the complete opposite with the web people here; everyone talks about everything. Everyone is supportive of everyone else. That was another reason Build worked really well the first year—the designers were happy to see an event like Build enter the community. The first year the attendee list was split between people from Belfast and people from the rest of the world. The 50 percent of local Ireland attendees were really helpful—they

helped nonlocals find the venue and recommended activities to do outside of the conference program. It's not just the Irish—it's the web design community. Everyone is really friendly, and we're excited to have people travel to Belfast and see what's going on.

There's an excellent web community here that we are proud of. We want others to see that.

Following the success of Build, you started publishing *The Manual*. How did it start?

I'd like to say that I had a grand vision or a great story about the beginning of *The Manual*. I was dissatisfied with design conferences, so I started Build—that's not very romantic. I'd love to say, 'It was divine inspiration.' I saw a problem, and I wanted to solve it. That's a nicer way to put it.

The Manual was originally going to be a printed companion to Build. It would include conference information, but also essays, illustration and more—a guide with editorial content. At the same time, I had been thinking about the current state of design writing, or lack thereof, of writing about web design and about the state of the industry.

Most web design-focused writing is practical, such as tutorials. That type of writing is great, and one of the reasons that techniques and web design as a practice move forward so quickly—because people write, learn and share. Jez Burrows and I started working out the idea for *The Manual*, and we realized that the web has reached a point of maturity over the past few years and decided that it's time to do some sort of reflection. We thought, 'It's time to publish proper long-form editorial essays with some heavier articles, about design-thinking, in relation to the web.' That's not to say that this type of writing wasn't happening before *The Manual*—it certainly was, but it wasn't collated or curated.

I went to Brooklyn Beta, Cameron Koczon and Chris Shiflett's web conference in New

York, and talked with people about the idea of the 'maturing web.' My particular gripe was that people weren't writing about the web in the right way. Conferences do a great job telling that story, but no one had put it into words.

We wanted to tell our contributors, 'Here's a bit of time; here's a bit of money; go think about that thing that you're passionate about. Go write about it, and then we will publish it for you.' We wanted to give people that opportunity. Ultimately, we decided *The Manual* wouldn't be specific to Build, it would be bigger than that. Jez and I just needed to figure out what it would look like. I was introduced to Carolyn Wood, writer, author and former editor at *Codex* magazine, at Brooklyn Beta, and our conversations cemented the form of the book. Then we launched the Kickstarter campaign, which wasn't necessarily a way to get money, it was more a way to find out if people wanted it. They said yes, so, we got enough money to start the first issue and get the ball rolling. The first issue is now in its second edition. We sold about 6,000 or 7,000 copies of the first issue. Issues two and three are still in first edition but are almost sold out.

Have you considered taking on a publisher?
No. I like self-publishing too much. We have a really tight grip on the production specifications of the book. It's not cheap to produce, and we specified every single thing. I asked Jez, 'If money were no object, what would you do?' He said, 'Let's expose book binder board, bind the spine partially, deboss the front, and choose the best paper.'

He knew what he wanted to do with the illustrators. I said, 'OK, let's do it.' We selected every detail. One problem with me as a person is that I like to work on my own. Apart from Kyle Meyer, who designs and develops the Build site, and Jez, who created the Build identity, it's often just me.

Do you consider working by yourself a problem, or do you think it's why you can accomplish so much?
I do think it's why I can get so much done. I love working with other people, but I like being my own boss. I like being the one who makes decisions. When it comes to things such as print specifications, I don't want to answer to anyone.

Do you consider yourself an entrepreneur?
I hate the word 'entrepreneur.' There's just not a good word for it. There are a lot of words that have been appropriated to explain things, and I think entrepreneur is one of them. I am sort of an entrepreneur. I dream up stuff I want to make and then go make it, which is sort of what an entrepreneur is, but I would never describe myself that way. I think of myself as someone who likes to make stuff.

I'm very lucky that Build has a good reputation, that people are crazy about attending, and that *The Manual* is selling well. I have the flexibility that if I dream something, I can just go do it. Resources such as Kickstarter help make that possible because I can see that other people want the same things I do. If I need to raise a bit of money to start something, I don't need to ask permission from anyone.

What are your thoughts on Kickstarter?
Once I had a successful Kickstarter campaign, I started to get a lot of emails asking, 'How did you do it? What's the trick?' There's no trick. The Kickstarter projects I've seen fail often have the wrong approach—they see Kickstarter as a big, infinite box of money, which it's not. I don't even see it as a funding platform. It doesn't replace traditional funding. People see projects such as the Elevation Dock, or Double Fine, and think, 'There are millions of dollars here, and I want some.' Kickstarter provides a way to figure out whether 800 people believe in something enough to support you. The money is just their way of saying, 'Yes,

do it.' The real value is in that support, not in the 25 bucks you get for your book.

Do you still do web design?

I don't. It's very time consuming. I like the making part, but my collaborators are better at it than I am. Better than I ever was. I recognize my weaknesses, and I like to bring people on who are smarter than me to do those parts.

People ask, 'What do you do?' If I want to give them a quick answer, I still say 'Design.' I am involved in designing my sites and in web design, but I haven't taken on client work since the end of 2010. I still design websites, but I don't take them full process. I get involved in the parts I like doing, and Kyle Meyer and Paulo Zoom do the rest — they are better at it than me.

Is writing a large part of your process?

I hate public speaking, so I started a conference, and I hate writing, so I started a book. I have some kind of sadistic tilt when I start projects because I really like to force people to do things that I don't like doing. I don't write. Since I started Build, I've become better at public speaking. Since I started *The Manual*, I have become a much better writer. I can recognize what's good and what's bad because I'm immersed in it.

Do your writers produce one-off pieces for you, or do they write as part of their practice?

It's a mix, and we do that deliberately. We like to pick people who are writing all the time, such as Craig Mod, who is writing for us. He'll pick an essay, work on it for a long time, publish it on his site and then as a Kindle single. He makes a real occasion of publishing a piece because he is a writer, and he writes really well. He understands writing as a discipline, and he's a publisher, too — he gets it. But we really like to involve other people who don't write as much or have never written at all.

The Manual, Lettering; Design, Dan Cassaro

That's when an editor comes in. Good editors can hold someone's hand and walk them through the process for the first time. Fortunately, we've never published a weak article. Everyone has delivered. We work hard to pick people who think really well.

Some people are better at putting their thoughts into words than others, and that's where an editor helps with the entire process. An editor can have a huge impact on a piece, and the reader never sees it. The editing process is completely invisible. It's very bizarre.

Do you give direction to your writers?
No. It's very free form. We've never done that with Build either. We don't pick a topic and have everyone talk to that topic. We pick smart people who do interesting things and ask them what they've always wanted to write about and ask, 'What have you been sitting on for a year?' Almost 100 percent of the time, people come back and say, 'I've been dying to write about this thing; do you think it'd be good for *The Manual*?' The best writing comes from authors who write about things they are passionate about. Much of the writing in *The Manual* is timeless because it doesn't discuss specific technologies, and we don't allow the authors to show markup or screenshots.

For *The Manual*, we want you to be able to read our essays in the next few years and have it all still make sense.

Many designers in the states are making the move away from client work. Is it the same in the web design community in the UK?
I don't like generalizations, but the goal of many designers is to offload client work and to have more control over what they're doing on a day-to-day basis. That typically means getting rid of client work. But, I know many designers who are very happy with client work and love working on something different every day. A lot of designers like the variety.

I don't think it's a New York or a San Francisco thing. I think everybody wants more control. There's a lot of potential on the web; we're really just getting started. There are a lot of success stories out there about people who have stopped doing client work and built something. That's motivating for a lot of people who want to have control over their time and get up in the morning to work on their own time. I don't know why anyone wouldn't want that. I don't think it's geographic — it's just everyone with an Internet connection.

What do you think is the most exciting thing about being involved with the web community now?
I have a mushy answer for that: the people involved. I love that I get to hang out with everyone. Build is a lot of work. I don't like to harp on about that all the time because I'm very lucky to be able to do it at all. The thing that motivates me is knowing that I will get to see everybody. The people in the web community, more than any other community I've been involved with, are so nice. The community in Belfast isn't unique; we have a lot pride in our little bit of the world. But it's not just our community; everyone on the Internet is nice and friendly.

Events such as Brooklyn Beta, New Adventures and Build bring people together to have fun. It's not like going to another bullshit conference. Everyone is just there to have a good time. That's the most exciting thing about the web. Not the next app that's coming out. I know a lot of interesting people working on interesting things, and that's exciting, but the most exciting thing is the people.

Nothing is more motivating than talking to people who are excited about what they are doing. I get to have hundreds of those conversations during Build. I get to meet friendly, excited people. It's so much fun.

Build Conference, Lanyards; Photo, Filly Campbell

Kyle Sollenberger | Cofounder, Seesaw | Lancaster, PA

Seesaw, Mobile Application

"Find people who are doing the things you want to be doing and reach out to them."

Kyle Sollenberger

Keep Moving Forward

Kyle Sollenberger took a bet on Twitter and won. He and his cofounder, Aaron Gotwalt, were having trouble tweeting from the same Twitter account, so he founded CoTweet, a business front-end for Twitter that allows companies' social media management teams to collaborate and tap into social media conversations in real time. He tapped a new market by solving his own problems.

With his new company, Seesaw, an application that allows users to make decisions with the help of their friends, he's back to solving problems—this time by asking others. Whether building products for businesses or for consumers, Kyle helps communities make life a little better.

Could you give us a little bit of your background and how you came to design? Have you always known you were interested in entrepreneurship?
My interest in design is less about creative expression and more about how people experience the world around them. Throughout my school years, I wanted to be an architect but quickly realized how the web allowed me to create virtual spaces in which people could interact with in minutes. Rapid iteration and user testing are much harder in the physical space. I wanted to move quickly, so the web won.

My parents instilled the entrepreneurial spirit in me, and after high school, I dove in headfirst. A couple of friends and I decided to start a small interactive shop where we created everything from CD-ROMS to magazine ads. One of our clients was a vertical market CMS provider. While working with them, we explored a potential merger that fell through, and I decided to go on full time as partner and creative director. At 20 years old, I was managing other people, some twice my age, and ended up creating more than 2,000 websites in my three years at the company. It was a great experience that taught me a lot about what and what not to do in business. It also helped me to land some great clients during my time as an independent designer, which supported my desire to dive into product work. I had stayed in touch with one of my previous business partners, Aaron Gotwalt, who was always shooting off new ideas. We began dabbling in side projects here and there. It was when we were trying to promote some of these projects that we discovered how hard it was for multiple people to use the same Twitter handle, and thus, CoTweet was born.

When did you realize you wanted to control your own destiny and pursue your own ideas? How did you weigh the risk involved with that decision?

The big decision point for me was when I decided not to go into architecture as a career path. I don't learn well in an academic setting, and college life wasn't appealing to me. Putting that together with the fact that to become an architect requires an inordinate amount of schooling, it was just out of the question. I didn't really ever weigh the risks. It was less a question of risk than it was a matter of believing in myself to accomplish whatever I set out to do.

How did you decide to collaborate with your partner, Aaron? Do you think it's important to pair a designer and a developer during a product's creation?

The best way to describe our relationship is that he throws the Play-Doh down on the table, and I squeeze it through the press. I think it's important that you have someone who will push you to be better. He does that for me.

When did you decide you should involve a business strategist? How did you find yours, and would you recommend other designer and developer pairs find someone to help them with the business side of things?

When we started CoTweet, there was an opportunity to claim our stake as the thought leader in a new space. The conversation had just started on whether businesses should be on Twitter, and we took a bet that they would. Jesse Engle was a master of relationships and had the business acumen that we needed to attract large companies. We knew where we fell short, and he filled the gap. It's not necessary for every startup, but it was absolutely necessary for what we were trying to accomplish. We couldn't have done it without him.

Can you describe the opportunity you identified and fulfilled with CoTweet?

There were two of us and one Twitter account. If we were having trouble, imagine what would happen when a large business with hundreds of people across multiple business units tried to do the same.

Do you have any words of wisdom or advice for designers attempting to push their products to market?

Stretch yourself. Believe in what you're building, and build it. A great idea is nothing without hard work. Attitude is everything.

Do you have any advice for how designers can develop an entrepreneurial spirit?

Read a lot and not just books about design. Read about business; read for fun; read about knitting; read about anything and everything you can. Find people who are doing the things you want to be doing, and reach out to them. Don't be scared; they're normal people, too.

Can you comment on the perception of design within startup culture?

Things are changing. Design thinking has been proven over and over again, and entrepreneurs are seeing the light.

Should designers found startups?

I don't think it's for everyone. Client work can be as rewarding as startup life for some, but there are definite trade-offs. Designer cofounders have a unique opportunity to shape the company and its culture. I also believe that when a designer has more skin in the game, they are more connected to the cause and therefore will create a better product. With CoTweet I wasn't just a designer—I was customer support, product, business and research.

You, Aaron and Jesse teamed up again to create and build Seesaw. How did you get the idea, and what problems or opportunities did you recognize?

Aaron and I had been throwing ideas against the wall for almost a year before we stumbled upon Seesaw. We thought we could make a go of it ourselves, but we quickly realized that we were missing the 'hustler' piece of the puzzle. Jesse brought that to the table in CoTweet, and we knew we needed him again.

Jesse came up with a great, new idea—Fab or Drab: a quick and easy way to rate what your friends ask. It's since evolved into Seesaw: the easiest way for you to get opinions from your friends when you need them most.

What do you envision for Seesaw's future?

It's a huge opportunity. Advertising is moving toward curated content. People continue to post more products online via Pinterest, Twitter and Facebook, and it's the perfect opportunity to capitalize on the 'purchase decision.'

How was raising money, building the product and shipping it different the second time around?

The first time was in early 2009, one of the worst times ever to raise capital. It took six months of hitting the pavement hard, with an idea that had a lot of momentum. With Seesaw, we were able to formalize the idea, create the prototype and raise a round within a matter of weeks. It was a world of difference. We also owe a lot to Jesse; he is a master at handling negotiations and relationships.

Seesaw, Logo

American Felling Axes, Best Made Shop Display; Photo, Sandy Soohoo

"I think that every business will succeed if the owner feels like there is no stopping it."

Peter Buchanan-Smith

Start Making

Peter Buchanan-Smith is passionate about products — and one product in particular, the axe. In 2009, he left behind a successful studio practice and launched Best Made Company with a single product, the Best Made American Felling Axe. Best Made has since expanded into a well-loved brand popular with high-end shoppers, outdoorsmen and the design community alike.

Peter took a risk for the chance to tell a story. He's grown the business from a company that makes axes to a brand that encourages the Boy Scout, adventurer and dreamer in all of us — and he does it for the love of the product and the chance to do it all.

Can you tell us about your background, how you got your start, and how you transitioned into entrepreneurship?
How far back do you want me to go? [laughs] I grew up on a small farm in Canada, it was relatively isolated, and it wasn't like I had much to do. I had to self-entertain. The obvious activity that I gravitated to was to make things. Or destroy things. One or the other. The farm was where that seed of 'making' was first sown, and I still feel like that's what I aspire to do — to just make things.

I studied fine art in college, and I got really frustrated with it. I thought I wanted to be a painter, but I realized that making art was essentially making things for myself. I didn't feel like I made anything for anyone else to appreciate or enjoy, or at least I felt that my making was arbitrary. I became part of a few tiny publishing ventures at a university in Canada, and I got hooked on the idea of mass-producing something. Publication design just seemed like such an alluring facet to 'making stuff.' The design was the place that I felt was the nerve center to any kind of publishing operation. If the design sucked, no one was going to read it. Then it became my mission to learn more and get inspired by great designers. I moved to New York to work in publishing. I started working for a book publisher and soon enough hit the wall in terms of where my personal ambition was concerned. There was no room for me. There were all these other people above me who we allowed, and paid, to design the most beautiful book covers. But I wasn't in that position, and I wasn't going to hang around and wait for someone to promote me, so then I went to the School of Visual Arts' MFA Designer as Author Program. What appealed to me most was the promise of a thesis that would actually get published, one that would see the light of day instead of ending up as a design experiment that gets put in a portfolio under the bed for the rest of your life. The MFA program offered what I had been looking for my whole life: to make something that would see the light of day.

I had lived and worked in New York for two years in the book publishing industry, and the idea of getting something published, or making anything real, seemed impossible. This wasn't my small town in Canada; this was the real deal. I pushed forward, and using a lot of the resources from the MFA program, which were invaluable, I ended up publishing a book, *Speck*. That was the beginning of my career as a designer/entrepreneur. That's the genesis.

What lessons or core values, or principles, did you take away from your previous career in publishing?
Right after SVA, I worked as an art director at The New York Times, but I always worked on side projects to maintain my sanity. Something I try to instill in the students and young designers whom I meet is this idea of doing a side project. No matter how small, it is always important. Remind yourself why you love design and why you're here to begin with. I think when you go to a corporation, and when you're entry level and just starting out, a lot is asked of you, and you can lose yourself and get washed up in it.

I never wanted to work in a design firm. I never wanted to have a designer or an art director looking over my shoulder. I wanted to work with people who didn't know anything about design. I wanted to work with editors and a team of people with different talents and skill sets—then together we would create something.

Going back to the idea of making. It's hard to think of The New York Times as 'making something,' but it really was. It's on a very large scale, but at the end of every day, there's a newspaper that comes out, and it would have my mark on it. And that was just so exciting.

One of the reasons we started Kern and Burn was to create a resource in which we could gather perspectives. We wanted designers to have greater access to the mentors, stories and inspiration that we as graduate students were fortunate enough to have. How important is it for a designer to get a graduate degree? And what were some of the mentor relationships that you received in grad school, and how important have they been to you?
It's a case-by-case basis. I firmly believe that most people probably don't need a master's degree to do what I've done or to become an entrepreneur. Sometimes I think a master's degree is almost antithetical to the entrepreneurial process. Getting my master's was good for me mainly in that I was kind of lost before I got there, and it gave me a lot of options. I could see firsthand stories of success and get inspiration.

Of the people who were an inspiration to me, the main one who has been a constant throughout my career is Maira Kalman.

She was my thesis adviser, and the work she did with Tibor Kalman at M&Co, and her whole outlook on life and creating and making has rubbed off on me in a huge way. Ever since I left SVA, I've been under her spell. I don't know a better way to describe it. I've been inspired, enchanted and very influenced by her. A lot of my clients have come by way of her, not that she actively sought them out for me. People such as Isaac Mizrahi, who I've done a lot of work for—he was her next-door neighbor. She has taught me a lot about the importance of being true to yourself and keeping things light and playful. I think that's really important. I also think that there's a duality to it; you need things to be light and playful, but you have to be super serious about them being light and playful. Often, it feels like everything has huge consequences but you have to let go a little bit. Especially as a designer when you're starting your own business, it's easy to get wrapped up in so many things that will just side track you. There are many distractions. Maira taught me that to persevere, it is all one big experiment.

Be Optimistic, Felt Badge

How important do you think business education is for a designer? Obviously, you wouldn't suggest that design students get an MBA when they're done, but do you think that business acumen evolves organically from side projects, or do you think it's something we need to be strategic about learning and teaching?

That's a really good question. If design is like a nerve center of sorts, what it can bring to any business is critical, and if in the right hands, with the right designer, it can be so powerful that at the very least, it can get something up and running. You don't need to know how to use QuickBooks or Excel. It's good to have a basic understanding of this stuff and an appreciation enough that you can bring people in to help you with it. I spent the first three years of Best Made Company totally flailing around with what I would consider the 'back-end stuff,' the parts of a business that no one ever sees. But I had my hand on the pulse and worked very hard at crafting all of the stuff that people do see. I don't want to sell the business end short; I think it's hugely important.

It sounds stupid, but as long as you're making money that's the most important thing—you might, because of your lack of business skills, lose it, but if you're a good designer, you can make up for that. Looking back, I feel like I've spent the last two or three years building my business plan in real time, and I think that's a good thing. Most people would create a business plan before they even opened their doors, but I'm glad that I did it this way. Now I've got the template, and the mold is cast. We are starting to embark on this process of finally writing our business plan, and it's going to be a lot easier for us because the business is there.

Who can write a business plan unless they have some real sense of what's going to sell? No matter how much experience you have, it is hard to know how anything is going to sell until you know how your brand is received and

Paler Male (redux), American Felling Axe

the message of what you have to say as a brand—unless you're designing software, or car parts or something. Best Made Company is much more nuanced. It's much more about this, for lack of a better word, lifestyle, or aspiration or attitude that people want to be a part of. To create that does not take a business degree.

The other thing that I want to say, that I think is so important, is whether your specialty is in business, design or whatever it is that you bring to the table, it's really important to remember that as an expert or as someone who has a specialty in something, you can very quickly become a technician. And that is the death of every small business.

It's so easy to get lost in a specialty, especially when you're an entrepreneur. You are running a small business; you're out on your own, and there's no structure. It's very easy to get lost and lose track of time. It's like being stranded on a desert island; I've seen it time and again. It's a trap that I constantly have to remind myself not to fall back into—the trap of only doing stuff that I'm really good at. Graphic design only occupies about 5 percent of my time, but that 5 percent makes it all so worthwhile. You have to be really disciplined in that sense.

The Best Made story seems to be directly related to your personal history and your passion for the outdoors. How have those interests shaped or infused the business? Did you intend them to, or have they been crafted into the story after the fact?
The business started at the height of the mortgage crisis and the economic meltdown in early spring 2009. My graphic design business was losing clients, budgets were being slashed, I had been working in the city for 15 years, and I hit the wall. I decided I really needed to look after myself. I understood that a client wasn't going to take care of me. I needed to not only look after myself in terms of putting bread on the table, but also look after myself emotionally and creatively speaking. There were a lot of people who felt this way and were ready to use the financial crisis as a source of change.

It is almost like an addiction working for clients. There's a saying that drug addicts will never recover until they hit rock bottom. It was like that for me. I started to feel like I could never do this on my own; instead of believing that, I just started the business.

My parents still lived up on the same farm that I was born on, and I would go up there three to four times a year. While all of this was happening—the economic crisis, the loss of clients, an extreme amount of time in the city combined with these trips to the farm—it was a whole collision of conflicts and ideas going on in my brain. I was at the point where I needed to reconnect with nature in the most basic sense.

I could sense that same feeling bubbling and simmering in the public imagination. I felt like people were anxious to get outside and into nature but didn't know quite how to do it—they just needed a little push in the right direction and some inspiration. I found that in the axe, in this tool that would be an evocative symbol for people. If they bought it, had it in their house, hung it on their wall, did whatever they wanted with it, even if they never even went outside, it would always be this reminder to them, this window into another world.

Did the concept of getting back to nature start when you discovered the axe? Or were there other keystone products that you thought about using first and then came to the axe?
The axe came first; the axe came before Best Made. I was invited to contribute some products to a gallery in New York. And at the time, I had some axes sitting in my workshop that I bought on eBay, and none of them had any kind of adornment. I knew that I didn't want to make an art piece for the show in a way

that I normally would or a way that I was comfortable with. I wanted to make a real product. I remembered that when I was growing up, my dad had an axe that had a yellow safety handle on the bottom of it, and it was painted on as a purely utilitarian function. For the show, I decided to take an existing object and then paint it. Those first axes sold pretty much instantly. I just put two and two together. My inclination for everything is, 'Oh, we can start a business out of that.' Rather than just keep painting axes, I decided, that no, this was an excuse to start a real business that's going to sell other products in addition to the axes. It's not like M&Co was started because Maira and Tibor saw that the future was in umbrellas, or paperweights or weird watches. They had a desire to communicate with people on a very substantial, meaningful level. They were working on expressing that sort of connection for their clients and then discovered that they could do it just as well, and they did. I feel like designers, just by virtue of being a designer, have it in themselves somewhere. A lot of people are terrified of starting a business. It's not easy.

I think that every business will succeed if the owner feels like there is no stopping it. The only way to get to that point is to be so in love with what you're doing that there is no such thing as failure. I said, 'Well if this project just ends up becoming me painting one axe a month for a friend and mailing it to them, then it's still a success.' A lot of people would consider that a total failure, but I remind myself of that. Once you wrap your head around what you think is the worst possible case scenario, everything else is easy. It becomes really simple.

The digital fabrication revolution has allowed many entrepreneurs to create products overnight. Why have you chosen to go the route of the craftsman, and why is that important to you?

I feel like I'm a Frankenstein of both the overnight and slow-growth models. I took an axe that was made by someone else, and I just painted the handle. The hard part was selling it and developing a catalogue and world around that one painted, simple axe. It was done overnight in a way. I had no business plan when I started. I literally painted 12 axes, photographed them, and two or three weeks later, I built an e-commerce site, and they were up for sale online. That's pretty fast.

It has been very slow to develop and craft some of the products that I want out there. That's what's been hard; it takes time and money, and that doesn't come quickly unless you're willing to sell half of your company or something, even if that were possible. But, I've learned a lot from my manufacturers. We work with a 140-year-old axe company that is still run by the same family. It is really inspiring to go down there, to watch them run machinery that was built 80 to 100 years ago, and see that they're not anxious about growing really quickly. To them, it is about long, sustained growth. No one is thinking, 'Let's get rich quick.'

I'd say that's the sad thing about a lot of products that I see out there that probably don't last because people came to it expecting too much, too quickly. That's the way we've been taught to think lately, that that's the way the world works, and if you can't make money, you can't be happy any other way. Well, if you work with a 140-year-old axe maker, that's actually not true. We're developing the notion that you don't have to have instantaneous, huge, obvious results all of the time. In the time that we've worked with this axe maker, we've only ever released two different versions of the axe, but it's a roller coaster every day with them. It's a roller coaster with all of our vendors, to just continue to develop the product, and to continue to try to sell it, that's the excitement. You think of slow-growth business like what we're doing, and you kind of just want to take a nap. But it's anything but boring and slow; I think it's fast and super exciting.

When you release new products, are you testing to see what is going to be well received, or do you have a pretty good idea of what's going to sell?
Right now I have a really good sense of what is going to sell; what is going to sell really well is always up in the air, and it always surprises me a little. We are focusing on some long-term development products, and we are growing into a business that's got a real core to it.

We've released a boot oil, a shepherd's mouth whistle — it's wonderful and wacky. I love these products, and I think they have a very important place in our catalogue, but along with other people's products, we are really building up the Best Made brand catalogue into something that we believe is great.

Wool Lumberlander Scarf, Best Made Accessory

How do you convey the backstory and the notion of optimism found in Best Made to someone in a few short sentences?

The slogan has become that, 'We are making tools to empower and inspire people, to get outside and use their hands.' That's one answer. Another answer might be that we are trying to make the world a much better place. That sounds so earnest and righteous, and I feel like every company would probably say the same thing—whether they believe it or are doing it is another question. I have a firm belief that quality products with amazing stories, even though they're material objects, and some of them are very expensive, can serve very valuable roles in our lives. At the very least, it's nice for people to question whether that's true. They can look at an axe, and they can say, 'Oh, I'm kind of horrified by that, and I'm never going to spend more than $100 on anything ever again.' Or, they can say, 'Wow.'

When I started Best Made, in the midst of a crazy economic crisis, I thought that if the shit hit the fan, and I lost everything, and I could only take one thing with me, that's what it would be; it would be the axe. I have always seen the axe as a very inspirational tool in that sense. It's the oldest tool known to mankind. It's actually the oldest art form as well, known to mankind. It embodies so much; it's a symbol of simplicity and virtue, but it also can be threatening and menacing. And I love that; it's a very loaded symbol.

You built your model around emotional connection with physical products. Do you think we can connect with digital products in the same way? Should the designers of digital tools or products think about that emotional connection and story as well?

Yeah, I wish that digital designers would stop trying to think that they can do everything—that using an app will be as rewarding of an experience as going out

and chopping wood with an axe. I could be wrong, but I don't think that will ever be the case. To me, the best designs of anything, whether they are digital or physical, are made by people who understand the limitations.

I think the digital world has gotten so overrun and cluttered with everyone out there trying to prove that they can do things that that medium simply can't do. But again, I'm constantly surprised and amazed what digital things can do, but it's always the simple things that amaze me the most. I feel like a company such as Google is always coming out with something that makes me say, 'Wow, they got it.' And the reason it's so good is because they understand their limitations, and they're not embellishing it with stuff that we don't need.

Field Rule, Best Made Tool

Bellini, Trilliny and Earl Grey, Wiloughby, Summer Crystals Collection

"We're always trying to think, 'How can we do good?'
and 'How can we have a bigger impact?'"

Neil Blumenthal

Change the World

Neil Blumenthal knows a thing or two about designing for the social good. For five years, as the director of VisionSpring—a nonprofit that works to bring vision to people without access to glasses—he dedicated himself to helping people who made less than $4 a day and learned about the eyewear industry. He used this insight to cofound one of the coolest and socially conscious companies around.

Warby Parker offers boutique-quality, classically crafted eyewear at a revolutionary price point—$95. Neil and his cofounders saw an opportunity to build a brand that made them excited to come to work — and at the same time, have a positive impact on the world. Contributing to the social good has never looked so good.

Did you and your three cofounders realize that your interests and passions would make for a great collaboration, or did you just have a great idea and decide that you all wanted to work together?

It was really organic. We were close friends, had similar fashion sense, and were complaining that glasses were too expensive, so the team was really built off our shared experiences and our personal bonds.

It wasn't assembled as an 'A team' because we had these very different skill sets. For example, it probably would have been great if we had someone who was a technology expert. But I think what it led to was us just building a brand that represents the four of us, and that is what has resonated with a lot of people, and it's the reason that we've been able to grow so quickly.

Can you describe your background and relationship with WP partner VisionSpring?

We owe a lot to serendipity, and we owe it to Wharton that the four of us were able to meet and build these great friendships. I was fortunate enough to be introduced to an eye doctor, through a family friend almost 10 years ago, and it was through that connection that I got involved with international development and started working at VisionSpring as the second salaried employee and pioneered a model to train low-income women to start their own businesses selling glasses to people in need. I did that for more than five years and expanded it to 10 different countries, and I gained a lot of experience that became really useful as we were building Warby Parker. First, I learned a lot about the manufacturing process. I learned that glasses aren't that expensive to produce, even good-quality ones, and I developed relationships with suppliers that we could then use at Warby Parker.

Second, I made contacts and built relationships within the optical community so that we could learn how the industry operates. One of the first things that Jeff, Dave, Andy and I did was really look at the industry dynamic. We discovered that there's one company in particular that controls everything — Luxottica.

They make about $8 billion a year in revenue, and they're vertically integrated, so they control the manufacturing of frames. They produce all of the big brands, such as Ralph Lauren, Chanel and DKNY. They outright own Oakley, Ray Ban, Oliver Peoples, Persol, Arnette, and on top of that, they've purchased all of the retail chains of scale — Lens Crafters, Pearl Vision, Sunglass Hut, Sears Optical and Target Optical. The icing on the cake is that they own the second-largest vision insurance plan in the country.

They can set the price point.
Exactly. We saw this great opportunity to build a brand that reflects who we are and could answer or correct that problem that we experienced, which was going into an optical shop and getting really excited about a pair of glasses and then walking out like somebody had kicked us in the stomach. We found that we could bring the price of a $500 pair of glasses to $95. But we still recognized that there were hundreds of millions of people who didn't have access to glasses, even at $95. We thought, 'How can we serve them?' Because at the end of the day, we wanted to build a company that we were excited to work at every day and have a positive impact. That's where the Buy a Pair, Give a Pair program came from.

The success of WP is two-fold; it's very successful in the fashion world and in the social design world. Do you think the company would have been as successful without the social initiatives?
The social initiative was part of our DNA from day one and just something that motivated us personally. I think that it has had a profound effect on our business because our story makes sense to people. We're offering a $95 product for something that is typically sold at $500, and that question automatically is well, 'Why?' And, 'How?' The why is because we personally experienced the effects of overpriced glasses, and we want to change the world.

We want to transfer billions of dollars from these big, multinational corporations to normal people. We have a history of doing good in the world. I had spent five years running VisionSpring, and this is something that is near and dear to our hearts, and that makes sense. The how is that we're able to design the frames ourselves and produce them under our own brand. We've made relationships with the suppliers that make the hinges and the screws,

and then custom-acetate and assemble the frames, and cut and etch the lenses, so we're able to bypass the middleman by having those direct-to-supplier relationships, and by filling orders online, we have direct-to-consumer relationships.

With backgrounds in business and international development, how did you decide to design the glasses yourselves?
I think while we haven't been properly trained, we each have a pretty distinct design sensibility. I have a little bit of experience designing a collection; while I was at VisionSpring, I learned how to do it on the job. And we would just draw references from what we like. We've often looked at what our grandparents wore, and now we produce a monocle that's designed after Andy's grandfather's monocle.

We think that we get the social impact and revolutionary spirit from our parents, who were part of the hippie generation, and we get the design aesthetic and the fashion sense from our grandparents, who were going to work every day in the '40s and '50s.

Winston Walnut Tortoise, Auteur Collection

WP has a really great relationship with its consumers. Is this something that you knew you wanted to build in right away in the business model?

One of our mantras is, 'Treat others the way we want to be treated.' That's pretty much basic etiquette. It's one of our core values, and it's something that we hire people and fire people based on; it's something that's just engrained into the culture of the company. When we were thinking about the process of buying glasses online, we thought, 'How would we want to do it?' We knew that we wouldn't want to pay shipping, that we would want the ability to return, and that we'd want the ability to try them on, so we created the Home Try-On Program. If we had a question, we would want to talk to somebody who was friendly, smart and empowered to make a decision to help us. Stuff that when I say it out loud sounds really basic, but just doesn't seem to be the status quo in the marketplace. We intuitively knew that there were a lot of other people just like us who wanted to be treated in the exact same way. Building great consumer relationships was infused within the company from day one, and when we hire people, we hire them based on whether we think that they're friendly, and whether we think that they can make good decisions on their own, because you know, we're not going to approve or disapprove whether to give someone a discount on a free pair of glasses—a customer-service agent needs to be able to make those decisions.

You learned design on the job. Is business something that can be learned on the job as well? Are there other resources for designers to learn about business?

I think the best business people and managers understand design, and I think the best designers understand business and management. There has to be a lot more cross-pollination. Perhaps the business managers aren't working with the designers enough to allow the designers to know what the top priorities of the business are and what the trade-offs are. Likewise, business managers probably don't fully grasp the benefits of good design, so both sides need to learn. We have an amazing senior designer who leads our design team, and we've recently hired an executive coach for her. We've done that for all of our senior managers. Leadership needs to be taught in every school, design, nonprofit, you name it. I think that there is a big hole in our education system—we are not teaching people how to lead. We try to focus on leadership at Warby Parker. We ask ourselves, 'How can we each help each other grow professionally and personally?'

There seems to be equal interest in Warby Parker from a high fashion and design standpoint. What was the strategy to position yourselves in the market?

I think it goes back to who we are and who we think our customers are. We think that they're diverse and multifaceted, and in general don't want to be pigeonholed. There are certainly folks in the fashion community who love fashion, but that's certainly not the only thing they love. They love design; they love art; they love an intelligent business model.

We tried to cultivate relationships with different communities, such as the design world, the fashion world, the nonprofit and social enterprise world, and the tech and startup community. I think that we're doing things that resonate with each of those communities. Hopefully we're able to serve as a case study that those communities can learn from, and likewise, we too extract so much learning from those communities. We sort of see ourselves as normal people in that we live in all of these different communities.

Are you working with VisionSpring to think of ways to continually push the social initiatives that you've started?

One of our other core values is innovation, and we always think that the envelope can be pushed further. VisionSpring is our primary glasses distribution partner. We work with other groups such as Community Enterprise Solutions, and they themselves are constantly innovating. VisionSpring recently developed a process in which they can bring precut lenses into the field and pop them directly into frames, which creates the ability to provide glasses on the spot in one visit. That's a really big innovation because it cuts down on the cost of having to visit a particular village twice. We're trying to do everything possible to help our nonprofit partners innovate. I've been talking to some folks at MIT who are developing a technology to do refractions out of your smartphone. That could be a game changer for our nonprofit partners. We're also one of the only carbon-neutral eyewear brands in the world.

We also are always trying to think, 'How can we do good?' 'How can we have a bigger impact?' I think that there are a lot of ways that we can have a positive impact that go beyond just getting glasses on people's faces—we're just getting started.

Whiskey Tortoise, Colonel Monocle

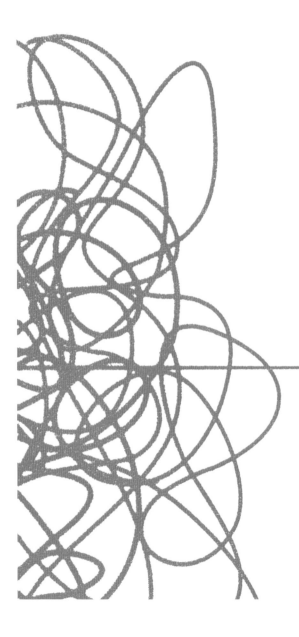

Armin Vit | Cofounder, UnderConsideration | Austin, TX

Brand New Conference, Website Detail

"People just want to be entertained...
They want a visual assault of stuff."

Armin Vit

Provide a Jolt

Armin Vit has been an avid contributor to the design discourse since he launched Speak Up in 2002. It was a web platform that searched for relevance in graphic design in its commentary on current topics. He has since cofounded UnderConsideration with his wife, Bryony, a graphic design firm and publishing enterprise rolled into one. It comprises a network of blogs, including BrandNew, For Print Only, Quipsologies and Art of The Menu, publishes books, and organizes live events and judged competitions.

Armin is one of the foremost critics on design today and continually challenges the design profession with each new venture.

Tell us why you started Speak Up.
I started Speak Up in 2002, when blogs were first getting their start. You had to be a real nerd to blog. It wasn't mainstream; people didn't really know how to do it, and there were no automated tools to help you get started. I was invited to write for Typographica, a typography-focused blog. It was fun, and I wondered whether I could do the same thing for graphic design.

When I started Speak Up, I just wanted to see what would happen. It was also a reaction to the wave of experimental design that exploded as a result of the web. Designers discovered that they could design something, put it online, and it would never have to exist in print. No one could design gradients and 3-D exploding polygons for print because they wouldn't work. I thought traditional graphic design should have a place online for people to talk about it.

Did you build it as an online platform to encourage more thoughtful conversation around graphic design?
At the time, 'more thoughtful' meant that I said, 'I hate this; this sucks, and the AIGA is shit.' In a way, I just wanted to get people's attention. I knew that I had to be a little edgy. People responded to that attitude and said, 'Hey, this blog has a fun vibe. It's like being at a bar with friends; we can talk shit, and no one cares.' Then after awhile we started to get more

serious and wrote more thorough, thoughtful pieces. We still had an edge but weren't as juvenile, and that's when we started to get more attention from the industry. All a sudden, Steven Heller and Rudy VanderLans were writing guest essays. But we still had no idea how to monetize it.

People would pull me aside at events and say, 'Armin, you have to figure out a way to make money off this.' And I said, 'No, it's not about the money.' And now, today, it's all about the money. Now that I made blogging my career, I need to see a return.

We had advertising on Speak Up, but it was minimal. We aligned ourselves with cool, young companies such as Veer, but we could never figure out a way to make advertising work. We didn't have the analytics then. We didn't know how many people were looking at the site. We launched Brand New and focused solely on sharing our opinions on corporate and brand identity work. It launched with 6,000 to 8,000 page views a day and has grown every month. Right now, the blog is up to about 60,000 page views a day. We now have large, concrete numbers to give to advertisers. We can understand our users and learn that 30 percent of our viewers are senior-level executives or 50 percent are freelance designers and so on. We have nice demographic breakdowns, and can ensure that advertisers get their money's worth and a certain number of impressions. Then we launched For Print Only, where we celebrate the reality that print is not dead and showcase the most compelling printed projects, and Quipsologies, where we corral the most relevant and creative online and offline bits that pertain to the design community. We built a network of blogs that was enticing for advertisers. From 2002 to 2007, Bryony and I had full-time jobs, and UnderConsideration was always a side venture. We realized that we could survive off the advertising and some client work. In 2007, we decided to see what

would happen if we made UnderConsideration our career path. For two years, we were running the sites and also doing client work. The moment we knew we could live off UC without client work was when we launched the Brand New Conference. The conference was profitable; we realized our audience was great, and we had created a franchise that was generating interest. That gave us enough confidence to fully go after it.

Is your book *Graphic Design Referenced* an attempt to capture the current state of graphic design, similar to the motivation for Speak Up? It reminds us, in concept, of the Walker Art Center show, *Graphic Design: Now in Production*.

That book took us a year and a half to complete, and it was really hard. We thought it would be simple. We write daily for the blog; we thought, 'How hard can it be?' But writing and designing a book are really different from typing away on a blog. Writing for the web is temporal. If a fact is wrong on a blog, someone will catch the error, and it can be edited. In a book, you have to tell the truth; you have to get the history right, and you have to make sure everything matches up correctly. You need a consistent tone of voice, across all pages, for completely different content. The process of researching, contacting and following up with designers is time-consuming. The book became more about project management and a decision to commit to it than about any grand philosophical idea. It started as a great idea, and it became a matter of logistics and just getting it done.

The book prepared us for our role on the curatorial team for the *Graphic Design: Now in Production (GD:NIP)* show in the sense that we knew how to work with designers and had experience getting permission and rights to work.

For *GD:NIP*, we presented the key identities of the last few years, which could be displayed in a museum setting, in a way that people would understand. Brand identity is just one layer of graphic design. We didn't want to talk only about specific design-centric identities—we wanted to reach wider audiences. We showed the Google doodles; people engage with that type of design every day. We took a step back and thought about the types of identities people can relate to in an accessible way.

Graphic Design Referenced was published in 2011 and doesn't include a section on web design. If you wrote it again, would you change the way you approached web work?
Yes, I would. The web has really grown up in the last few years. Part of web design's evolution is that we can now embed fonts that look good. We're no longer limited to Arial, Verdana and Georgia. Graphic designers have built sites either by themselves or with developers for more than a decade now, and the web has matured a lot; aesthetics have become more memorable. The absence of web design in our book sparked a big argument. People wanted to know where all the websites were; they wanted to know where sites such as Amazon.com were. I go to Amazon.com to shop. The design of the site doesn't move me to do anything. Yes, it works nicely, but it doesn't inspire me.

Speak Up, Logo

How can I compare that to Milton Glaser's iconic Bob Dylan poster? His poster captures an artist and culture. Amazon captures your data.

Self-publishing is a great entry point for designers to move toward entrepreneurship. You self-published *Flaunt*—do you prefer self-publishing to working with a publisher?

Yes, I do, because I like to have control over what we do. We published three books with publishers, one with Rockport and two with HOW Books. The process is fine, but there are moments when not having the final call takes its toll. For instance, when a publisher tells you that the marketing department doesn't like your cover. And they ask you to come up with another five options. I wanted to say no, but I didn't because I had a contract that said I had to make the changes. I thought the cover design I showed them was perfect, but a marketing team didn't think it would sell. Self-publishing is nice because I can show a design to Bryony and say, 'Do you like it?' And she says, 'Yeah, it's great; ship it.' It's a really smooth process.

Did you figure out distribution on your own?

Distribution is the hardest part of self-publishing. We didn't realize how hard it would be. As a self-publisher, you have to move the product. It's one thing to have a large enough audience to easily push out 1,000 books. It's another thing to package those books, put them in a box, put a stamp on it, and mail them. That process is a huge wake-up call. Our bathroom doubles as our shipping department. It's piled with boxes. Our closet and kitchen are full of *Flaunts* and Brand New Awards and FPO Awards books.

What portion of your day do you write for the blogs?

About two hours in the morning—5 a.m. to 7 a.m. is a good time because it's quiet; the kids are asleep, and I can get things done for the day. One week of posts for FPO and Art of the Menu requires a lot of prep work and code. I used to write for three or four hours a day, and then try to come up with new content. Our interns are able to help with those tasks, and they've taken a huge load off us.

Do you get submissions, or do you search for new content yourself?

All of the blogs' content comes through submissions. We get tips for Brand New. We have a submission form for FPO. For Art of The Menu, we ask people to send us menus they've designed or see.

You wanted to take the design conversation to a broader audience through Speak Up. How did you feel when you realized it had transitioned from being like drinking beers at a bar to a serious platform?

I was 24 when I started Speak Up. I was young, and I think a lot of the tone reflected my age. At that age, you think you're the best and the world owes you something. You think that you know everything and no one else knows anything. But, when other magazines asked me to write for them, I decided to take my writing more seriously. I became less abrasive and more considerate. It went from being really juvenile and opinionated for the sake of it to something a little more controlled. That was around 2005 or 2006. Now, we have a great audience that in part comes to the site for the sarcasm and irony that I write with. I have more confidence, and I'm more comfortable with the fact that I can balance being snarky and provide an opinion that's based on 10 years of knowledge.

I'm not the smartest guy. I'm not the best designer in the world. But I pay attention to design, and I've worked with great brand and identity designers, so I can channel that knowledge in an entertaining way. I went back a bit to sarcasm, but I'm also a bit more mature.

Speak Up ran its course in 2009 and exists now as an archive. Is its end a reflection on the state of design discourse today?

To be honest, I don't think anyone wants to read more than 250 words. The main nucleus of graphic designers today doesn't give a shit about graphic design writing. Or about criticism. People just want to be entertained. They want more 'stuff' that they can draw from and put into their work. They want a visual assault of stuff, and long-form writing just doesn't do that. I only get through articles because I want to get to the point. I don't get a jolt from reading long-form writing. Twitter and Facebook give a jolt. People don't even read Brand New, and I only write two paragraphs. I don't ask for much. I know firsthand how much people just want to look at things and react.

Do you think it would be beneficial for the design profession to provide context to the 'visual assault of stuff' out there?

I think if you're being optimistic and positive, you could say that people can tell what a piece is about without the context. You could argue that people are more literate about reading into a piece of graphic design and that there's a greater general understanding of what makes something work. The more pessimistic view is that we just go through visuals at a speed that doesn't allow us to think about or understand them. The ideal outlook would be that as designers, we create a balance between thoughtful responses to work and pure appreciation of aesthetic. Some things are worth knowing more about, and some things are just worthwhile to look at and say, 'Yeah, that's pretty cool,' and move on. You link to it on Twitter and move on. Hopefully you get a retweet, and then you're happy.

How do you view the power of a tool such as Twitter? How does it help designers?

I want to make a T-shirt that says, 'Content is Prince, and Retweet is King.' That's what matters.

2011/12
FPO
Awards

UNDERCONSIDERATION

For Print Only Awards, Book Cover

Even if what you tweet is not something that you did, it's just something you linked to—if you can get 100 retweets—that gives you more power than if you actually make the thing. That mention is more powerful than anything you might make. It's funny how that dynamic has changed.

Do you consider yourself a designer first or an entrepreneur?

I'm definitely a designer first. Design is what I love and what I write about. I'm a graphic designer first, a writer by accident and an entrepreneur by necessity—because I need to make money. All of my work goes back to graphic design. I've taken on some client work that landed on my lap by accident, and it feels good to take on that work, to not have to worry about launching something new or where we will store products in our house. It feels good to do a logo and let the client worry about implementation. It's a reminder that design is what I like to do and what I'm good at doing. Most people think I'm just a critic. Critics don't 'do,' they just write. We've never pushed our design side and said, 'If you like what you read here, hire us to do a logo.' We don't do that.

Did you do identity work before Brand New?

Yes, but I didn't intentionally go after it. My second job was at a small design firm, and we created brands for small companies. When I worked for Pentagram, we did a lot of identity work, and I really enjoyed it. I saw how the conversations happen with clients, how a team effectively works with clients and sells ideas. Identity work is just something that happened.

You said critics don't 'do.' We want to encourage practicing designers to write more. Any opinions on new platforms?

I have no idea because we haven't seen it. No one wants to read someone's blog. Frank Chimero is good, but I still think people don't want to read someone's thoughts.

What about collected opinions, such as those presented in *The Manual*?

All that format does is rehash old methods that the design field already went through. It worked for a while, but it doesn't anymore. On the web, no one has the attention span. No one wants to spend 30 minutes reading on a website, probably not even on an iPad.

Maybe video could work—a combination of the spoken word and visuals. If you can put together an 8- or 12-minute video to cover what you might in a 10,000-word essay, people might watch that. It's more entertaining. You just have to entertain people.

What about conference lectures, and recorded talks and presentations?

Take CreativeMornings, for example. Those talks are short, sweet, entertaining and to the point. TED talks are so popular because they are 20 minutes long. TED speakers also happen to be the smartest people in the world, but still, it's the format.

I love the PechaKucha format, because it enforces a time limit, and as a viewer, you know what you're going to get. People need to work within a certain framework. The best excel, and everyone else bombs.

Maybe 'new platforms' just means 'new constraints.'

It's kind of sad to admit. But I think that's where we are at the moment. It will take a lot for designers—and people in general—to move back toward extended reading and then reference those things they have read in a printed article that they write.

Last time I opened *Eye* magazine, I thought, 'Really? I have to read through all of this?' In the past I devoured it. I used to love *Eye*; I would read the whole thing in an afternoon. Part of the change is that I've become accustomed to wanting a new mode of short and sweet things.

For Print Only Awards, Website

When you monetized your blogs, there weren't many examples of other sites that had successfully done it. Do you have advice for those who want to monetize a blog now?

It's not easy, especially if you want to try to make a living. You have to reach a certain number of required page views to join ad networks, such as The Deck. The most successful blogs today have very specific niches. They exploit the heck out of a certain niche and become really good at it. For people to come back to your blog day in and day out, you have to define your niche and find ways to continually make the same topic interesting.

Even with an amazing, receptive audience, it's really hard. You won't make a lot of money unless your site pushes a million or 2 million page views a month and you can sustain that number. For full disclosure, we get around 1.75 to 2 million page views per month. We charge $2,000 a month for an advertising banner. We accept a maximum of five advertisers per month. For the most part, we make $8,000 or $10,000 a month. To make those numbers, we need to continually get 1.5 million views a month, and that's an enormous amount of people that requires a lot of attention from us. I have to put fuel into the fire every day. People want us to do more posts on Brand New. I can only handle one post a day; I'm only one man. We could build more to the blog and develop it, but it's already too much.

What about FPO and Art of the Menu?

For Print Only has been going for a few years now, and Art of The Menu launched in 2011 in a total spur of the moment. I saw a nice menu, then I saw another one and thought, 'We can build a blog around this.' In two or three weeks, the blog was up. It didn't have a plan. We let our ideas grow however we can, so we can react to what's going on. Instead of looking to expand, now we are trying to get better at what we already do. We're trying to push *Flaunt* a bit

Flaunt, Book Cover Detail

more and maybe start a series of workshops. I like the idea of creating a model that can be replicated in any city.

Have you figured out different ways to engage your audience in the conference and awards setting?

The Brand New Conference has a narrow focus. It is all about logos, branding and identity. The Brand New and FPO awards are also focused. We've found a niche; we know our audience, and now we can build things for them. Take The Dieline. God bless Andrew Gibbs and The Dieline. It took me 10 years to build what he was able to do in one year. The Dieline gets 2 million page views a month, and he has a conference and awards. Much of creating a successful blog lies in being in the right place, at the right time, with the right thing. For Andrew, it was packaging design. He represents the epitome of keeping it simple. He posts pretty pictures as big as he can possibly give them to you. If monitors were bigger, he would give them to you bigger. There's almost no editorializing; he just says, 'Here they are, beautiful examples of packaging design.' It's instant gratification.

He made a book that's essentially the website in print. Have you thought about that model?

Why turn something that already exists better in web form into a book? The Brand New awards are successful because of their contrast to the Brand New site — they only celebrate the best of the best.

On the blog, we show examples of brand identities that are good and bad. The most popular posts are the bad ones. That's what people want — the bad. We only give the best designs awards because it gives people a reason to buy the book. If we published the worst designs in the book, no one would buy it. No one wants a book with the new Gap logo in it.

We do what works best for whatever medium we use. My advice is to figure out what works in what medium.

What are your thoughts on designers who keep their heads down and work versus those who share their thoughts and opinions?

Designers should keep their heads down and work, and hustle, but come out for air. If you just work, work, work and look up five years later and everything has changed, that's not good. You have to throw it all on the wall and see what sticks. It's good to have a balance. It's good to put your head down and work, but balance that, and expose yourself; see whether you're right or wrong. See whether people agree. Then go back inside; take the feedback and continue. It's a balance of both methods.

You aren't afraid to take a critical view toward work. People with huge followings online have an opportunity to take a stance and often don't. What are your thoughts on being critical online? Do you think it's a reflection on society that we all just want to be nice to each other?

It doesn't pay to be a bitch. I'm not mean-spirited, but I can do it. If I don't like a typeface, shit, I don't like it. You might like it, but I don't have to like it.

A lot of it comes down to the way you say it. I've come face-to-face with people whose designs I've ripped apart, and they've been mad. It's about the work. It's not about them. It's just about the work.

Any favorite design entrepreneurs?

Peter Buchanan-Smith. When he came out with the axes, I thought, 'What a hipster thing to do.' But he has created an amazing lifestyle brand. He sells beautiful things. He turned the image of a Williamsburg hipster in the woods with an axe into a beautiful thing. He's a great example of someone who's monetized a passion.

Chris Coyier | Founder, CSS-Tricks | Palo Alto, CA

CSS-Tricks, T-Shirt

"Fall in love with your idea, not the idea
 of being a founder."

Chris Coyier

Fall in Love With an Idea

Chris Coyier is a blogger, author and speaker. He studied graphic design in college, spent a few years working prepress in the printing industry, and dabbled in web design. Now a full-fledged web craftsman, he has written and published Digging Into WordPress, *shares his insight on CSS-Tricks.com, travels the country and speaks about front-end development, all while running CodePen, a front-end code-sharing site, and ShopTalk, a web design and development podcast.*

Chris has pursued his passions, built vibrant web communities, and continues to create web services that give back to designers. Designers use the tools he creates in the things they build — for Chris that's the biggest motivation of all.

Can you tell us a bit about your background and how you came to web design and development?
The direct jump into web design was in 2007, when I left my job as a prepress operator to work for Chatman Design, a small design agency in Madison, Wis. I had tinkered with websites for years in my free time, so when it came time to interview, I had a few personal projects to show, and that was enough.

My whole life has led to design. I was a computer nerd kid all through middle and high school. I started college in computer science and math, nearly finished that degree, until I became jealous of the relaxed lives of my art- and music-major friends, and I switched to art. Now my life is a nice balance between computers and art.

CSS-Tricks.com was the best resource we used when we learned to design and develop for the web. Can you describe what motivated you to put so much time into creating an educational resource? Have you always enjoyed teaching others? Do you view it as a gift to the community in a way?
It's not as altruistic as that. One of my first attempts at building websites was a small network of blogs based around Adobe software support. I was reading guys such as Darren Rowse of ProBlogger and wanted in on the

get-rich-blogging thing. It wasn't an awful idea, but my heart wasn't in it. CSS-Tricks was the worst performing of my blogs, but it was the only one I liked writing for. The others quickly fell away. Through renewed focus and hard work, CSS-Tricks grew up. I feel differently about it now. Now I'm more addicted to the community aspects. I write, and I get immediate quality feedback. People comment; they share it, and they use things I teach in the things they build. That's a pretty powerful motivator. It's bigger than money. The get-rich-blogging thing turned out to be more like live-comfortably blogging.

The site started as a side-project while you were working. Did you plan to monetize the site from the start, or was it something that came organically as you saw the increase in demand for your content?

The plan was to monetize right away, but that didn't work out so well, and the site ran the first few years with no ads at all. The first several ads I put on there were for companies that contacted me directly. I managed it, incorporated their ads into the theme, invoiced them, the whole bit. That became more of a hassle over time, and I switched to BuySellAds, which has been great. Lately the scale has been big enough I've taken to managing some of the ads again. Funny how that works.

I've only recently started relying on CSS-Tricks as more than a side project. I decided it was time to make a run at working only on my own projects and see if I could do it. The first thing I did was redesign CSS-Tricks. It needed a redesign anyway since there were so many underserved areas of the site. But instead of just redesign in hiding and slap it onto the site one day, I recorded myself redesigning the whole thing so I could turn it into a learning experience for everyone. I used Kickstarter to fund it, and my backers received access to the redesign videos. That turned out very well and made the first year of going it alone much more comfortable.

Do you consider yourself a design entrepreneur? Have you always wanted to provide educational resources and be in ownership of your work?

I don't really consider myself an entrepreneur. It might just be the word, though — it sounds too fancy for me. I like working on stuff that is fun and that people will like and use. Things that I take pride in. My dad is a garbage truck driver and president of his local union. Is what we do really that different? We both work on stuff and help people when we can.

Many startups are a turn off to me. They say, 'UsemeusemeUSEME.' Then they shut down. It shocks me. There is no pride there, no belief in what you are doing. I associate that kind of thing with the word 'entrepreneur,' unfortunately.

From the start, you've been a huge advocate of WordPress. What prompted you to turn your knowledge into *Digging Into WordPress* as a book and a site?

It was a bit random. Jeff Starr contacted me about the general idea of writing a book together. Interestingly, the majority of projects I work on start as unfocused collaborations that gain focus over time. We decided on WordPress as a topic as we both had blogs, but they weren't quite the right outlets for writing about that topic. We both had experience and things to say about WordPress, so it was a good fit. I also always wanted to design a book.

Side projects have always been a big part of your career. How do you approach a work-life balance, or are the lines intentionally blurred for you?

Intentionally blurred is a great way to put it. I enjoy the computer things I do, and I enjoy the noncomputer things I do. I enjoy the work things I do, and I enjoy the recreational things. It all kinda squishes together nicely. When I'm home visiting, my step-dad will often come into the room and say, 'Are you on the computer

again? What are you doing? Working?' He's both
bewildered that I spend so much time in front of
a screen and legitimately interested in what I'm
doing that second. I often find it hard to answer.

What does a normal day as Chris Coyier
look like? What percentage of your time is
spent educating yourself, educating others
and actually practicing design?
Email is a big part of it, which I'm sure is the
same for everyone else, and of course bumming
around on Twitter. I don't feel overwhelmed by
it though. I actually rather like it. I do need to
get better at closing that Gmail tab and Twitter
client for longer periods though.

ShopTalk, Logo

A good part of my day is spent on CSS-Tricks. I write and update articles—at least half of my time is spent updating old stuff. I shoot videos, jump into forums and do site maintenance, such as fix bugs and update ads. I also respond to support requests from users who write in with problems with the site.

Some days are ShopTalk days. We record live once a week on average at 10 a.m. In the morning, I prepare for the show. Then the show, which takes about two hours between the preshow, show and postshow material. Then I write the notes for it. While I'm in that mode, I usually deal with the communication and advertiser stuff for the show on those days. That can easily kill a day.

These days, I'd say the biggest chunk of my time goes to CodePen, which is straight up design and development, with a little community work. It's a three-man team with Alex Vazquez, Tim Sabat and myself. We're putting a ton of time into CodePen and hope to make it the best front-end code-sharing site ever, as well as a strong business.

The CSS-Tricks screencasts are one of the ways you set the site apart from other tutorial sites. How did you decide to start doing screencasts? We assume it is a lot of effort on your part to produce them.
It's simultaneously easy and hard to work on screencasts. Easy because I usually prepare nothing, do no editing and do no promotion. Easy because when I meet people in real life who have liked CSS-Tricks, they always mention the videos. Hard because analytics suggest hardly anybody watches them. Hard because it's a bit difficult to think of things that make for good videos. Hard because I can only do them from my office instead of from anywhere, like writing.

I've essentially decided to keep doing them but only once in awhile, when I happen to be home and with good idea in hand.

You often speak about web design and development. How important is it to you to engage the larger design community?
I like speaking at events because I get a kick out of it. I try to share some small things that have helped me, and hopefully I can help some of the people who listen to me. I try to stay away from the really high-level philosophical stuff, unless it's a simple way to frame a practical problem or solution. Making the web a better place happens person by person and site by site. There is probably some metaphor here about pebbles and rivers and stuff.

Did you move to Palo Alto to be closer to California's startup culture? Has being surrounded by the startup culture influenced or changed your practice at all?
When Wufoo was bought by SurveyMonkey, part of that deal was the team coming out to Palo Alto. I was glad to come; it's quite nice in Palo Alto, if pricey. I don't find myself too affected by the 'Silicon Valley' thing. The same movies play here as everywhere else. People drive the same cars. They sell the same cheese. Serve up the same Internet. The notion that you gotta live out here to do a startup is wacky to me. I've been to tech events all around the U.S., and the startup spirit is strong all over.

CSS-Tricks is an amazing resource for the motivated designer who wants to learn web design. Do you have advice for designers who have entrepreneurial ambitions?
The thing that you want to build should be your drive. Say you have an app idea that needs a log-in system. You should learn to build that log-in system because you need it for your app. Don't learn how to build a log-in system because you think you should, or because you think it's generically good for business. Don't learn Python because you think it's pre-req for a tech startup. Fall in love with your idea, not the idea of being a founder.

CSS-Tricks, Website

Jen Bilik | Founder, Knock Knock | Venice, CA

Hand-Lettered Series, Sticky Notes; Illustrations, Kate Bingaman-Burt

"Part of my life goal has always been to exercise both the right and left sides of my brain—as business and creativity do."

Jen Bilik

Value Your Audience

Jen Bilik does it all. She is the founder, owner and self-prescribed "head honcho" of Knock Knock, the irreverent stationery and gift company she launched in 2002. She's grown the business from a line of a few cards with witty punch lines to a $10 million dollar company that has produced products for small boutique shops and major retailers such as Target, Urban Outfitters and Costco.

The best designers and entrepreneurs identify a problem and craft solutions to solve it in a smart way — often, they do this simply by observing everyday culture. Jen saw big-box retailers' shelves devoid of intelligent humor, and she stocked them with smart wit.

You studied English, worked in publishing, and started Knock Knock based on your personal energy and humor. Do you consider yourself more of an entrepreneur than a designer, or are you just Wonder Woman?
Ha! Flattery will get you everywhere. I consider myself a writer, designer and creator first, and an entrepreneur and businessperson second. When I started Knock Knock, I don't know that I considered myself an entrepreneur or businesswoman at all. I certainly had no idea what I was getting into or what it would take to make this thing fly. At that point, and for a bunch of years, the gulf between the No. 1 and No. 2 identities in my mind was vast. Now the entrepreneur identity is close on the heels of the creative identity. It wasn't until about six years after founding Knock Knock that I finally felt qualified to run it and to manage all the functional groups. It's such a school of hard knocks — hey, I totally didn't even mean to pun that — entrepreneurship, that by the time you're not sucking so hard at it, you're kind of bruised and battered, which results in your feeling more of a claim on the entrepreneur and businesswoman classification because it has cost so much to earn it. My unofficial title has always been 'Head Honcho.' It's on my business card and my email signature. People love it, and I still like it, but I adopted it early on in part because I didn't feel comfortable calling

myself 'CEO.' Now I feel every inch of my CEO-ness and have no hesitation signing, say, legal edicts with that title. It's interesting, though, that the more successful the business becomes, the less I am seen as a writer or designer. Journalists and book writers don't seem to see me as a writer, and designers don't seem interested to hear what I have to say about design other than how it applies to product — and more often, they'd rather hear about how to take a product to market than they would about the design behind it. I was recently chosen to host a design conference, but the leadership changed, and I was deselected for the position because I was 'not a designer' — at least that's what they told me. I would love the opportunity to talk more about what we create and how we create it. Part of my life goal has always been to exercise both the right and left sides of my brain — as business and creativity do, as well as both to write and to design. I love not having to choose. I have a fantasy of simultaneously seeking an MBA and an MFA — in fine art, not design.

What or who inspires you in the design and business worlds? How do your interests outside of design influence your practice and business pursuits?
Creatively, I'm most inspired by renaissance creatives who've managed to work in multiple disciplines as well as make products that work in the marketplace. You know, creativity plus real-world imperatives. The Eameses, Tibor Kalman, Terence Conran, Martha Stewart, despite the sad deterioration of her brand. I find the intersection of business and creativity really fascinating, especially coming from people who've had to put it all on the line — not just the creativity, but the capital and business success to get it out there.

I cowrote the book *Todd Oldham: Without Boundaries* with the designer, Todd Oldham, and he was a great inspiration to me. Not only does he work in multiple disciplines, but he's one of the kindest, brightest, most generous, successful people I've ever met. Everything Hella Jongerius makes turns me on. Droog is invariably witty and socially on point. Fine artists would probably be the other inspiration category; I spend a lot of time in museums and art galleries. I also really appreciate reading about the experiences and approaches of other businesspeople. One column I love is the Corner Office series in The New York Times. There's also a collected book — *The Corner Office: Indispensable and Unexpected Lessons from CEOs on How to Lead and Succeed.* I'm kind of an omnivore intellectually and creatively. I read a lot, and I respond to high as well as low art. Reality TV is my friend. I mean, where else would you hear a Real Housewife of Atlanta say, 'Irony is so ironic'? I take a little something from everything.

As a businessperson, because a lot of the skill set doesn't include capabilities I'm naturally inclined toward, I suck the marrow out of others' experiences and advice. Because Knock Knock's products derive a lot of their conceptual and comedic impact from social observation, society informs me.

Your copywriting respects your audience's intelligence and wit. Did Knock Knock begin when you observed an opportunity to fill a void in the market, or did it grow organically?
Though I wasn't really enough of a businessperson to consciously fill a void in the marketplace, one of my main early motivations was that there didn't seem to be many products for smart people. By 2002, when I started Knock Knock, I was keenly aware of the practice of dumbing down and homogenizing for the mass market — lowest-common-denominator type of stuff, and nothing with a distinctive voice or point of view. Big-box retailers were all-powerful; nothing could offend, and there was very little smart wit out there — since then,

however, that sensibility has exploded. I figured there were enough smart people out there to support one small, irreverent company that told the truth and sometimes deeply offended, say, hypocrites. And is it really the worst thing in the world to have to look a word up in the dictionary? Or on your digital device? So in retrospect, I guess I did observe an opportunity to fill a void in the market.

IN THE LOOP

OUTSIDE THE BOX

I'M NOT HERE RIGHT NOW

ON THE SAME PAGE

I NEED COFFEE

LEAVE ME ALONE

I'M ALWAYS RIGHT

NOT ENOUGH BANDWIDTH

I NEED A _____

WHAT IS IT THIS TIME?

PARADIGM SHIFT

!!!!!!!!!!!!!!!!!!!!!!!!

Office Speak, Rotating Stamp

How has your role within the company shifted since founding Knock Knock?

Before Craig Hetzer, our publisher, joined the team, the earlier senior creatives and I had worked really hard to formalize the conceptual approach to Knock Knock's writing and aesthetic. It's not too different from creating a style guide. And if someone is asking you the right questions, or if you're encountering the right teaching situations, the descriptions of how to do it start to flow. And I think the DNA of the Knock Knock brand is pretty strong.

It's been a major strategic initiative for us to build a brand and creative team that isn't dependent on any one person, that can perpetuate itself indefinitely—kind of like the wall around the Spanish city of Toledo, about which it is said that every stone has been replaced, but it's still the same old wall. The company doesn't have much value, i.e., to be acquired, if it's got single-point failure with one superstar, whether myself or Craig. That said,

Slang Flashcards, Card Back

it's absolutely difficult to give up control. I don't find it so difficult when I believe in what's being done, even if it's not how I would have done it. What's tough is when I feel a project or strategy is going in the wrong direction. Sometimes I assert myself strongly and sometimes I don't, and I don't always prove to be right. Rather than the pain of giving up control, I think I struggle more with missing the actual doing of the creative work. The concepting—some of which I still participate in—the writing, the designing. I'm much more of an executive creative director now or perhaps a creative gadfly—I'm often the one asking the tough questions about concepts and designs. My distance from the day-to-day of the projects gives me a bird's-eye view that can be very useful when we're testing concepts.

Have you built a business that balances cultural observations with dedication to the craft of design and beautiful production?

Short answer: Yes. Caveat: I am very proud of our manufacturing department and the physical outcome of our products, and our amazing team works very hard to make that the case; however, with mass production, there are lots of things we can't do that I miss—such as choose beautiful paper versus using generic paper that differs only by weight; letterpressing and screen printing; anything handmade. I had originally wanted Knock Knock to encompass both, but I don't think that will be possible unless at some point we can set up a very different division, but even then, the scale of that division would be so much smaller than the scale of the rest of the company that it wouldn't deliver enough revenue to be a good business decision.

In addition to being beautiful, your products are witty and a delight to engage. How do you create a lighthearted culture? Do you only hire funny people?

It's great to hear that we're achieving what we set out to do. I wouldn't actually call our culture lighthearted. We have too much to do to be lighthearted. But I would say that we're informal and funny and free-spirited, and we like to have fun. We've tried to implement some formal procedures to help underscore that—outings, certain brainstorming approaches, etc.—but those tend to fall flat. Most people at Knock Knock have good senses of humor, but that doesn't necessarily mean that they'd be identified as the funniest people at the party. What's important is that they're smart and that they get the Knock Knock approach and can execute against it. Comedy as work is just that: work. There's a lot more banging it out, revising it, then revising it again than you would think.

In many ways the digital world has provided an opportunity for print design to make an impact through material choices. Is Knock Knock committed to physical goods? Where do you see opportunities for designers to delight their audiences by providing tactile experiences?

Knock Knock is definitely committed to physical goods, but we're also excited to start branching out into digital, not by doing the exact same thing in digital that we've done with paper, but by viewing the two as separate media. Makers of physical goods have to keep defining what it is that physical goods do best, versus what areas are better done digitally or by any other available resources. Fighting the inevitable—and innovations that do things better are generally inevitable—is just an exercise in frustration and eventually failure.

Is writing as much a part of Knock Knock's design process as the aesthetic process?

I would put that differently. At Knock Knock, product starts with concept. The concept often encompasses both the writing and the design, and sometimes the two grow together rather organically. Our concepts tend to be a bit more writerly, though, perhaps because concepts are

Slang Flashcards, Card Front

often best expressed in words. We focus then on how the aesthetic can either pull against or underscore the concept—do we want it to go with the grain of the writing or provide tension against it? Sometimes we'd like to do more complex designs, but those would compete too much with the writing. With both writing and design, however, the concept is the first thing, and then both go into execution phase.

What is your favorite thing about being in control of your own career?

I can't say I feel like I possess a large deal of control. In some ways, as an employee, you have your area, however small, that you control. You can control how much you go along with or fight the powers that be. And you have the control of being able to leave and get another job. As an entrepreneur, however, you're more exposed and vulnerable to multiple forces, many coming from outside the company, so you have to balance where you can lead versus where you must react. That said, I think my favorite part of being in charge at Knock Knock is that I can be decisive, and that the decision I think is best can often rule the day. Indecision and debating something after it's been decided drive me crazy. You should give due consideration to a decision, but when the time comes to decide, decide then move on. The strategy part of the business is pretty amazing, too—the fact that you can sit with really smart people and think about what to do and where to go next. There are also some things I'd like to do with my 'career'—I haven't called it that in a long time!—that would benefit Knock Knock but are somewhat outside it and certainly fall outside the business's day-to-day urgencies. I'm just now starting to have the time to approach them, but I can't wait to do more of those projects.

What was the biggest risk you took while building the Knock Knock empire?

The biggest risk was probably financial, sinking all my financial assets into the company. And I did a terrible job of managing expenses and manufacturing early on, which resulted in unprofitable early years.

What was your most important failure?

My most important failure probably had to do with a fraudulent manufacturing broker who stole from us. I allowed that to happen by breaking or not following a number of business rules: Always have things in writing—e.g., contracts; understand where the incentives lie, and protect yourself accordingly—(i.e., if someone gets a percentage of cost, they're incentivized to drive the cost and quantity up) don't let personal relationships cloud business—he [the manufacturing broker] had been a mentor to me, and we had become very good friends; don't put all your eggs in one vendor/supplier basket; and always solicit competitive bidding.

Do you have any advice for designers looking to start companies and move away from client service?

Do one or the other. I've rarely seen a company that can do both, especially equally well. I've seen product companies that take on a few clients and graphic designers who license out a few products, but they're such different business models that I've more often seen them crash and burn—versus Kern and Burn. I don't think you can just dip your toe into the product waters, unless you do it via licensing. Carrying inventory and fulfilling orders is just an entirely different activity and financial setup—not to mention it requires some very different skill sets. My advice would be either to shut down one business before you start the other, or have a very clear plan of how you're going to do both, specifying what percentage of time and money will be devoted to each, and how you'll manage resources, both human and financial, for the two and perhaps a plan to phase out of client services over time.

Squid-o the Squid, Clump-o-Lump Stuffed Animal

Tad Carpenter | Designer, Illustrator | Kansas City, MO

Sad Santa, Illustration Detail

"When we are doing something we love,
 we tend to do our best work."

Tad Carpenter

Love It, or Leave It

Tad Carpenter lives his life by a simple motto,
"Love it, or leave it." He is an illustrator, designer
and teacher living in Kansas City, Mo.
He has illustrated and designed several
children's books, including the, I Say, You Say
book series, which teaches children visual
literacy, and his latest work, Sad Santa, *which*
tells the tale of Santa's post-holiday blues.

Tad's love of storytelling and the spirit of play
are evident in the whimsical worlds he builds.
He recognizes the value and importance of
self-initiated work—it keeps him hungry, and lets
him explore and remember that he loves to make.

Can you give us a bit about your
background and how you came to design
and illustration?

I feel extremely lucky with how impactful my
childhood was on myself as a designer. I grew
up the only child of two artists. My mother is a
fiber artist who dyes her own wool and creates
large rugs and textile pieces, and my father is
an extremely talented illustrator and art
director. These two people, like most folks,
really shaped how I see the world. My father
has been an illustrator, writer, art director and
designer for Hallmark Cards for nearly 40 years
at its world headquarters in Kansas City, Mo.

I literally got to grow up in the halls of
Hallmark. I remember having interactions with
some of the most talented artists in the world
as a small kid at Hallmark Cards. I still to this
day have a drawing on my wall that Paul
Coker—of *Mad* magazine fame, and he was a
character designer for the beloved Claymation
Rudolph the Red-Nosed Reindeer Christmas
specials—did for me of Alfred E. Newman.

Another beyond talented person I got to
spend time with growing up at Hallmark was
Gordon MacKenzie. Gordon was one of my
father's best friends, and the two of them
worked together for years. Gordon's title at
Hallmark was 'Creative Paradox,' a vague title
that he really embraced. He was a liaison
between the chaos of creativity and the

discipline of business—something that Hallmark has always struggled with, as well as countless other companies of its size. Gordon would eventually go on to write *Orbiting the Giant Hairball*, which talks about the keys to creativity in the workplace, among other things. Something I took away from him and his book and still take away from Gordon and my Dad is the unbelievable importance of play. Play at home; play at work; play as much as you can. When we are doing something we love, we tend to do our best work. I try to never lose sight of why I do what I do. As a child I loved to make. That has never changed.

Kansas City is a nice place but not necessarily the first place we'd think of as the home of a successful illustrator. How has the city affected your career?

I actually hear this quite often. When I have a new client especially. They'll say, 'Where are you from? Kansas City... no way you are kidding?!' For a long time I thought I was going to leave Kansas City. My wife and I both are designers and both just knew and assumed we were on our way to another city. But as time goes by, I don't think I can leave. I almost feel a duty to this city to stand up for it, almost like a mini ambassador for KC and the Midwest in general.

With that said, I totally understand where people are coming from when they are taken aback when they hear this is home base for me. But a lot of people are unaware of the creative energy and talent Kansas City has, and has had, in the past. I mentioned Hallmark Cards' world headquarters being located here in Kansas City. Hallmark employs hundreds of designers, illustrators, copywriters, stylist, photographers and art directors that they recruit from all over the world. Some stay long term and some do not, but many stay much longer than they ever imagined. That is a small example of why I think KC is such an untapped creative area—so many people do great things here, and I really

feel that Hallmark and its roots have a lot to do with that.

Like all people who are self-employed in some way, I could not do it without technology. Ninety percent of all my clients are not from Kansas City. I do a lot of work in the publishing industry, so I spend a lot of time in New York. I do work in the music industry with clients in Los Angeles and brand startups from all over, such as Atlanta and San Diego. It would be really hard to reach those people without technology.

Do you consider yourself an entrepreneur?

I do. Each day as a designer who runs his own studio and maintains his own creative well-being, it really is the ultimate test of entrepreneurship. It's amazing how much time can also be devoted to aspects of our profession you never imagined doing—writing proposals, invoicing, pitching... taking out the trash. But having control over everything you do is quite comforting and liberating.

I would never have it any other way. I think having to hustle keeps you fresh; it keeps you young. It truly is my passion. If I had free time, I would be doing the exact same thing as I do day in and day out.

You put an emphasis on being first and foremost a storyteller.

I think a lot of us designers and illustrators are storytellers. My clients are all very diverse. From branding projects for restaurants to construction companies to tech startups and then to children's book publishers, magazines and apparel companies. All of those clients have a common need—they either have a product or an idea that needs to be shared. That is where we as creative makers and storytellers come into play. We help tell their stories.

I started writing ideas and concepts for children's books as far back as I can remember. As I have gained work and connections in the publishing industry over the years, I started sharing these ideas with editors and art directors. This past year was amazing when several concepts of mine were acquired from publishers and will be released internationally. I have a four-book, young-reader series being released with Little, Brown and Company. It is a series that will help to promote the importance of visual literacy in young readers.

I also wrote and illustrated a holiday-themed book titled *Sad Santa* that is published through Sterling Publishing. The books are super fun and a dream come true but so very different than a client project. I had to really get people excited about these projects, and teach and share with them their value—which can be fun and challenging in its own right. But being an entrepreneur means stepping out on a limb—stepping out on a limb and seeing whether it can support you. That idea in and of itself is exciting.

Sad Santa, Illustration Detail

Have you always wanted to be in ownership of things and tell your own stories?

I have. My father really molded the way I see the world and the way I create within that world. He has illustrated dozens of children's books. I got to grow up and watch him work and sit back and say that is exactly what I want. The fun, whimsical world I attempt to create is a product of my upbringing. Telling stories and expressing ideas is part of that same upbringing.

How do you balance your client work with the time and energy you put into your self-initiated projects?

This can always be a hard balance, but for me, I have recognized the value and importance of self-initiated work.

Small, self-initiated projects, such as a print or a poster, or larger, more focused projects, such as a book proposal, are what keep me hungry. These are what keep me always wanting to get better. Self-initiated projects also allow you to explore and play without consequence. There is no client telling you no, and no art director saying it should look like something else you made. It's just you and your idea.

Do you have any advice for young design entrepreneurs who are pitching their ideas and voice to the world?

For me, it has always been about being honest to who you are as a designer and ultimately to who your client is. Know what your client stands for and what they are expecting. It's always good to exceed expectations but never good to go around them. A thought that I remember Gordon MacKenzie saying was this, 'The only way to be original is by knowing yourself.' That speaks volumes.

Also, do not be in a hurry. I feel like when I was younger, I wanted immediate success. Still to this day goals take time. So rarely do they just appear. Good things are earned not given.

What is the biggest risk you've taken to get where you are? Do you have a favorite failure?

I think being a designer in general is a pretty big risk, every day. We sit and make things all day and then send them out in the world for people to see and use and criticize.

Everything we make and do gets judged. That is a pretty risky gig if you ask me. On a more personal note breaking out and working for myself was a big risk at the time and the best thing I ever did. More recently, I purchased a little plot of land and am designing a home and office in downtown Kansas City. A big risk, but we have to step out on that branch to succeed.

What is the best part about being Tad Carpenter?

Oh, wow. I am not sure. I just feel so lucky to be doing what I truly love for a living. I think at times we lose sight of why we got into the profession we did. We get stressed and forget to step back and look at what we are all doing. I love to make, first and foremost. Remembering that is important. If we ever lose sight or forget that we should love what we do, it might then be time to do something else. I live my life by a simple motto: Love it, or leave it.

Tad's World of Whimsy, Illustration Detail

Don Clark | Cofounder, Invisible Creature | Seattle, WA

Sasquatch! Music Festival, Toy Detail

"The biggest risk—and fear—was just starting out as a
new company, hot off the heels of a successful one."

Don Clark

Create What You Love

Don Clark and his brother, Ryan, knew exactly what they wanted to do with their lives when they were kids—they knew they wanted to create and to do it with precision and imagination. In the early '90s, the duo fell in love with punk, hardcore and metal, created a band, got signed and toured the country. In 2006, they opened Invisible Creature (IC) to build a company suited to their diverse interests, which range from music to toys to design.

They make time to pursue all of their passions at once and have discovered that their investment in personal projects leads to more freedom.

Can you give us a bit of a background on yourselves and how you came to be Invisible Creature?
Our grandfather, Alfred Paulsen, was an illustrator for NASA for 30-plus years. From early on, we were enamored with the fact that grandpa got paid to draw. That's where it all started. Ryan and I never wavered from that notion, knowing that we wanted to follow in those same footsteps. We were just drawing all the time.

Invisible Creature was born in the winter of 2006, shortly after the demise of our first company, Asterik Studio. We wanted to focus on illustration and packaging but also not limit ourselves to any category of design or style. We were conscious in picking a name that best suited our company now and for the future.

How did your interest in punk culture, the DIY scene and experience as musicians help you build the skills to exist as design entrepreneurs? Do you consider yourselves entrepreneurs as well as designers?
We fell in love with punk, hardcore and metal in the early '90s. Shortly after that, we formed bands, got signed and toured the nation.

During those years we met some great people, who turned out to be valuable contacts. When we set out to start our own company, we had a list of folks we could call on.

We had always considered ourselves artists and never really thought about being entrepreneurs. But looking back, I guess that sort of went hand in hand for us. We just wanted to create things we enjoyed.

What led you to turn your passions into a business for yourselves, first at Asterik Studio and then the decision to form Invisible Creature?

In 2000, my friend Demetre Arges and I landed our first real 'design job' at a tech company here in Seattle. We'd spend the day surfing K10k and just dreaming of owning our own studio — as I imagine many folks do in jobs like that.

Six months later, we got laid off. We were sort of thrust into making a decision at that point. We had both come from the music industry and wanted to make a go of it in the realm of design for music clients. I was doing album packaging and Demetre was doing web design. Ryan joined the team, and it was a go. We had a previous relationship with Tooth & Nail Records, and they graciously gave us a contract to work on a certain amount of projects for them. That's where it all started.

What is the collaboration like as brothers? Do you have as much fun as it looks?

Oh, we have fun. We always got along as kids, and it's the same as adults. The secret ingredient might be the fact that we couldn't be more opposite, but that has given us a solid mutual respect for each other. If we both had my personality, we'd be doomed. And vice versa.

How did you juggle a successful career in a metal band and design? Were you designing on the road with Demon Hunter?

It wasn't easy. In 2009 I decided to step down, so I could hit reboot and focus on IC and my young family. We actually never could design on the road. Even in a tour bus, there just isn't enough space — it's like a traveling hotel room

Sasquatch! Music Festival, Toy Set

with 10 smelly guys—or privacy. It's essentially impossible, so we would shut down the studio every time we hit the road. That was never an easy thing to do, so I had to make a decision. After eight years, it just felt right to move on. Ryan's the lifeblood of the band. Now I can just sit back and cheer him on.

When did you begin to transition your illustrations into vinyl toys? Was this a strategic step or a natural progression for your business?

We wanted to do toys for years but had been waiting for the right partner. Super7 reached out to us in 2010, and the rest is history. In my opinion, they are—and have been—creating some of the coolest characters and designs in that toy market. It was an easy choice for us. Plus they're just great folks.

The Leroy C. toys are self-initiated projects. Can you describe what it's like to see an illustration of a character come to life as a three-dimensional object?

As a toy collector and fanatic, there is a huge satisfaction in seeing one of our characters come to life. In creating the characters, we draw turnarounds for the sculptors. Front, back and side profile. We get updates on the sculpt and weigh-in with notes, and it goes from there. Honestly, Super7's sculptors are so good, we rarely have much to say. They knock it out of the park each time.

Are you interested in creating design products outside of client work? Do the vinyl toys provide a secondary income?

Absolutely. Personal projects allow us to experiment a bit and oftentimes lead to more client work. It's cyclical in that way, and we value them as equal. Income derived from posters, prints and toys usually goes right back into making more posters, prints and toys. That's just part of the fun.

The Sasquatch festival posters and toys are amazing. Can you describe how your partnership with Live Nation came to be?

Thanks! The partnership is actually with Adam Zacks, who created and books the festival. He's a good friend and tends to place a lot of importance on the artistic face of the festival. We're very thankful for our relationship and the opportunity to create something new each year. We had talked about creating a Sasquatch figure with Adam, who is also a toy collector, throughout the years. So for the 10th anniversary, we decided to just go for it. We started working on character concepts a year before the festival to give us enough time for toy production.

What is the biggest risk you've taken to develop Invisible Creature? What is your favorite failure?

I think the biggest risk—and fear—was just starting out as a new company, hot off the heels of a successful one. Would this new venture be as successful? Would we fall flat on our faces? When we had formed Asterik, I was newly married with no children—young, hungry and ready to tackle the world. With IC, I had two children and much more to lose if the company failed. Stepping out on your own while supporting a family—and without a regular paycheck—that's a scary place to be. Six years later, we're thankful that people are interested in our voices as artists.

My favorite failure? In the beginning I would say yes to every project that came in the door for fear we might not make enough to keep the lights on. The irony is that taking on too much work will oftentimes kill a studio. Luckily we made it out on the other side.

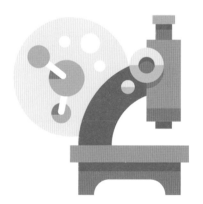

Jessica Hische | Illustrator, Typographer; Cofounder, Title Case | San Francisco, CA

Daily Drop Cap Alphabet Detail, "A" through "T"

"A designer is anyone who sees the world around them and tries to make it better through whatever medium he or she can."

Jessica Hische

Determine Your Own Value

As design's resident multitalented "designistrator," Jessica Hische is many things to the design community. She writes transparently about design and the creative process; she starts side projects, such as The Daily Drop Cap, Inker Linker and Don't Fear the Internet, that are as beneficial to the design community as they are fun, and she puts her whole self online and into her work. She runs Title Case, a collaborative studio with Erik Marinovich, and hosts workshops and events that teach others about lettering and type.

Whether Jessica brings a creative community together in her daily work or brings self-authored projects to life, she creates valuable resources for other designers.

We appreciate that you're willing to talk transparently about topics that others might think are risky and to share your perspective. Do you consider yourself a voice for the design community? How does your writing and design practice influence or benefit one another?

I do consider myself to be a voice for the design community, and I think the main reason why I've had such a positive response to my writing and side projects is that I'm not trying to be an academic or wax on about design theory. I offer practical advice and insight, albeit from a limited perspective—my own. Theory has its place, but I know that I and many other designers would sometimes rather cut to the chase when it comes to insights into the industry. I think, too, because I have dabbled in several realms of design and art—graphic design, lettering, type design, web design and illustration—I offer a different perspective than people who talk about singular industries. The main thing that I try to convey in all of my writing, and what I constantly reiterate when public speaking, is that it's OK to not know what you're doing, as long as you're self-aware and trying to improve. Also, that even though you can specialize professionally, you should never stop learning about everything else around you, if only to be able to delegate well and respect people in related industries.

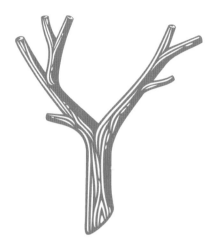

You've often described yourself as a 'designistrator,' reflecting your unique approach to lettering, illustration and design. We find the shift in personal definition an exciting reality for many of our peers. What does the definition of designer mean to you?

The further I fall down the creative rabbit hole the more I see just how different the realms of our industry are. I use the term 'designistrator' a lot because I have a background in design, but most of my client work falls more in the illustration realm. Most people look at lettering and think it's most closely related to design because words are involved, but it's much more closely related to illustration. How I define myself changes almost every year, as I discover what it actually means to be a letterer, typographer, graphic designer or type designer. Most recently, Typographic Artisan has become a title I've liked, though it doesn't capture the side-project entrepreneurial side of what I do. When you wear a lot of hats, it's hard to sum up what you do in a word or two.

'Designer' is a pretty broad term, so if I'd have to define it, I'd probably say that a designer is anyone who sees the world around them and tries to make it better through whatever medium he or she can.

Do you consider yourself an entrepreneur? How important is it for designers to be educated in business?

I absolutely consider myself an entrepreneur, though I don't think my entrepreneurial projects will ever make me a millionaire. Most of my ideas are geared toward a very specific group of people, and rather than focus my time on making revenue models, I focus my time on making something useful, or just beautiful and fun. I think it's essential that all designers get some training in business, be it through their university studies or through on-the-job experience. It's tough to sell a business course to design students, since many of them are so portfolio focused they'd be hesitant to fill a precious elective with a nonstudio class, but even a two-day workshop would make a world of difference to so many young designers graduating college. Half the battle is planting the seed, so they can seek out their own knowledge, and the other half is coaching them to acknowledge that what they do has value, and that they are in charge of determining their own value.

You've started quite a few side projects that have become beneficial resources for the design community, such as Inker Linker, Should I Work For Free?, and Don't Fear the Internet. Have you always wanted to give back to the design community?

Most of my side projects have started off as resources I wish existed for myself. Every time you think to yourself 'if only 'blank' existed' write it down. Chances are, there are a lot of others who think the same thing, and if you feel strongly enough about it, it's a great place to start when thinking about side projects. I've always been a bit of a teacher. I think part of it comes from being an oldest sibling, much of it from being a resident assistant in college, and the rest is empathy. I'm not that far removed in years from students, and I definitely remember what it feels like to not know where to start when you want to find something or learn about something.

Your authenticity and transparency in both your personality and work are refreshing. How important is it to share your process as a human being and designer?
Sharing your whole self online and in your work has pros and cons, but to me the pros far outweighed the cons. When I graduated, everyone wanted to set up a studio under a different name than their own. They wanted to be treated as an agency rather than an individual. This is really useful if the clients you want to attract are those who want an agency behind the work, but for me it became really important that people know me before they hire me. It can be really hard to develop a relationship with a client to the point that you don't question each other's feedback and know that you're not being made to run around a hamster wheel to please some cost-analysis person behind the scenes. I think putting myself out there has helped clients feel like they know me before they make first contact and maybe made them more likely to contact me over someone with similar work but less transparent of a personality.

It's also been wonderful to meet strangers who feel like they know me already. I can ask them questions about them and not have to go through the whole 'so what do you do' robotic introduction that happens at design events. I feel like old friends with people instantly, and strangers write me as if we've known each other our whole lives. It's wonderful to have every email feel like it's written from an old friend and not from a stranger. I'm a people person. I love hearing everyone's stories; I love making others feel enthusiastic and encouraged about what they're doing, and I love living my life as me and not some polished version of myself.

Daily Drop Cap, "Y," 4th Alphabet, "O," 2nd Alphabet

How do your side projects influence the way you think about client work?

My side projects have led to a lot of my client work, but the way they affect my thinking about client work is that they definitely take the pressure off to have each new client project be a beautiful manifestation of all my hopes and dreams. Most of the client work that I do is for advertising and book covers, and while book covers allow you to be pretty creative, most of the work I do for advertising means illustrating someone else's vision. The side projects keep me sane, allow me to exercise parts of my brain that don't get used as much during a lot of client work, and let me relish client time as 'making-awesome-pretty-things' time.

You say that you want to make more self-authored things. Have you always wanted to be in ownership of your own products?

To me, the biggest joy in creating self-authored projects is the ability to conceptualize, write and make artwork. Writing is something I love to do and have loved all my life but never really felt like I had a proper outlet for. Self-authored side projects become the perfect place for me to stretch my wings, be silly and irreverent, and show the world I can do more than draw curly cues.

Today, we consume so much design online, and much of it is presented out of its original context. Do you think that viewing this work out of context is dangerous?

I absolutely think that context and provenance are important, but I also appreciate the value in being able to consume beautiful artwork quickly, if only as a quick pick-me-up when you're in a work slump. I don't have an 'inspiration folder' on my computer, nor do I actually use sites like FFFFOUND! or Pinterest actively. If I were in the position to hire other illustrators, I might use them more, but for me, the real usefulness of these kinds of sites isn't the literal cataloging for future reference, but

Daily Drop Cap, "T," 4th Alphabet

the general impression and small nuanced details I might notice while perusing. In my article, 'Inspiration vs. Imitation,' which a few people skimmed through or misread, my main point is to have a lot of influences rather than just one or two, and that if you're going to work from sources, make sure you can still make it your own. By not working directly with sources, I draw from memory a lot and almost never am very close to the original set of things that inspired a piece because if you've ever tried to draw a room or friend from memory, you know how much idealizing and imagination goes into your drawing. If you're a blogger or anyone who reposts artwork from others, you should absolutely do your due diligence to make sure you get content from the right source, link back to the original work, and above all, make sure everyone is credited properly and that you have permission to repost. The problem with miscrediting and loss of context isn't the fault of the consumer but of the curator, so as an online curator, you must do your best to make sure that images don't lose their context.

The Daily Drop Cap helped you establish yourself as a freelancer. How important is it to be known for something?

When you're starting your career, it is so much easier to get the ball rolling if you can create something for people to remember you by. Daily Drop Cap was a huge version of the kind of promo all students try to make when they graduate. It wasn't meant to be a promo, but it ended up being a hugely successful promo for me. I became known as 'That Drop Cap Girl.'

If that title remains 10 years from now, I might reconsider whether I think it's smart to have such an easily definable shtick, but I know that as my client work and side projects evolved, my one-sentence title will evolve as well. It's fun to think of how people would describe you in one sentence and figure out whether you love your title or need to do something to change it.

Do you think it is beneficial for an illustrator to have a recognizable style? We could see it being beneficial to get work but potentially a hindrance to experimentation?

It is absolutely essential for an illustrator to have a recognizable style in order to get commercial work. There are very few illustrators out there who can switch up their styles often, whose clients trust that whatever they produce will be amazing and smart. As established as I'm becoming within the industry, most clients still reference previous work when hiring me, and if I do experiment, even with something as small as using less drop shadows or vignetting, generally people freak out and make me add it back in. You're hired based on previous performance, and if you can prove that you can perform perfectly in any style, you might not need a distinctive style, but very few people can do that.

Designers get up in arms about style, and every time I write about it, I'm greeted with hostility. People say things like, 'Well, if others are ripping off your style, it probably means you're outdated and should find a new style.' To me, this is like saying that once your car has a scratch on it, it's time to buy a new one. Style does not apply to design. Sure, there are designers who are known for working within certain styles, but you have a lot more flexibility than illustrators, and hopefully your topmost concern is making something appropriate for the client. If you find yourself working within the same style all the time, you're either working for very similar clients or not doing design that is appropriate for the clients you work for.

You are represented by Frank Sturges. How did you decide being represented would be beneficial to your career, and would you recommend it to other illustrators breaking into the business?

I reached out to Frank because I knew a few artists in his rep group at the time—friends from the Philadelphia illustration scene. Starting in design, I didn't really know that you could be a successful illustrator without a rep, as everyone I knew who had success was represented. It ended up being a wonderful decision since Frank really did help me get a lot of work when I was starting out. I remain thrilled with my relationship with him, though now he's more a sanity keeper than promoter. I would definitely recommend having a rep to illustrators starting out, especially if you don't have a mentor within the industry to help you through pricing and contracts. Just make sure that if you do choose to find a rep, you find one who cares about you and your career and isn't just trying to make a buck. You want someone who will tell you to turn down a job because you're too busy, or that it's OK to not want to do work for the tobacco industry, even though it pays tremendously well. Anyone you do business with should treat your relationship as a partnership, and good partners care about each other's well-being as much as they care about the success of the business.

You have the freedom to be selective about your collaborations and partnerships. How do you choose which projects to invest in?
Most of my collaborations and partnerships first start with a relationship with the people involved rather than a love of the project. I have so many of my own side projects going on—some of which are in serious need of updates and love—so any new side projects are entirely centered around friends and peers who I admire or causes that I believe in.

You were a part of a talented group of designers and illustrators at the Pencil Factory in New York, and you've recently moved to San Francisco and started Title Case. How has being surrounded by a brilliant network of people changed the way you think about your life's work?

Surrounding myself with motivated and talented people has been really important to me since college. No matter how independent you consider yourself, you are definitely influenced by your peers in some way, and I wanted all of that influence to be positive, nonjudgmental and most of all, motivating. I've seen how surrounding yourself with the wrong kinds of people can be incredibly detrimental to your success in life, whether they're actually causing harm in your life or mistaking motivation for brownnosing. Surrounding yourself with creatives helps you put your own work into perspective and pushes you to move forward. The Pencil Factory wasn't unlike living in the college dorms, if you saw everyone else was still working at 10 p.m., you wanted to keep working, too. More practically, having people around whose opinions you trust to critique work is awesome.

Daily Drop Cap, "X," "Q" and "L," 1st, 6th and 9th Alphabets

Riley Cran | Cofounder, Lost Type Co-op | Vancouver, BC

THE QUICK BROWN

FOX

JUMPS OVER THE LAZY DOG

Muncie, Font

"It has been a goal to increase the base
standard of design quality in the world."

Riley Cran

Dare Yourself to
Change an Industry

Riley Cran saw an opportunity for a new method of font distribution and took it. He cofounded Lost Type Co-op, a pay-what-you-want foundry (the first of its kind), and in turn, provided a way for members of the design community to acquire fonts within their means.

Lost Type's business model has paid off, and the site has become a thriving marketplace, where designers can try their hands at type design—by submitting designs of their own—and purchase unique and high-quality fonts from peers. Riley has created a valuable resource made by designers for designers.

How did you find design?

I come from a family of graphic designers and illustrators. My parents met in art school, and together they ran their own brick-and-mortar design shop, which supplied props to the movie industry. I grew up in an atmosphere of creating things; I've never known anything different.

Can you talk about the origin of Lost Type and the concept for a pay-what-you-want font foundry?

The idea began with some of my first professional design experiences, where I ran into a common roadblock: 'I don't have enough fonts.' You're working along, and you suddenly have a need for a condensed sans serif, and it isn't in your font book.

I looked around at the commercial foundries, and their stuff was gorgeous, but the price points drifted into the $200 to $400 range, which was beyond my reach for some of my first design jobs. I was discussing this issue with a friend of mine, and he said, 'Well look at this.' He spun his laptop around and showed me that he had pirated a large number of gorgeous fonts. I couldn't deny that they were beautiful, but I also couldn't bring myself to pirate them. Guilt overwhelmed me when I thought of the hard work these type designers had put in and how valuable the fonts would be to me in practice.

That put a kernel of an idea in my head. I wished that I could acquire beautiful fonts for a price within my means, without feeling guilty at all. I ended up purchasing books on type design instead and began to learn how to draw my own letters. The need remained for beautiful typefaces in my everyday work, but I wanted to educate myself and eventually learn to draw my own display faces and typefaces.

I was having a conversation one night with my pal Tyler Galpin, a web designer in Toronto, and we were chatting about beautiful script logotypes. He mentioned Kiehl's, which is undeniably beautiful. I mentioned the Ball jars' logotype — those glass mason jars — and I went looking for a specimen of the logo. What I found was an ad from the late '40s, which featured this secondary lettering in a very angular condensed style. Most likely something that was drawn specifically for this ad and never even built out into a full alphabet. We both fell in love with it immediately, and I began drawing it up.

You set out to resurrect it?
I figured I could draw it up and distribute it for free to the community online, and Tyler said he'd design the site through which to do that. We dared each other to do it in one day, and 24 hours later, we had this very basic display face up for download.

After staying up very late, I sat and watched as hundreds of people downloaded a copy, and I began to think that there might be potential in this sort of 'rescuing' of old lettering, and that this might be a way to form the 'pay-what-you-want' font foundry that had been brewing in my head for some time.

How did you build up your font directory?
I immediately started contacting my designer friends, asking who would be interested in designing a font for the collection, and what their ideal experience of acquiring a font would

be. I used these interviews with professional designers to formulate a series of rules and regulations as to how Lost Type would work. For instance, as manager of the project, I wouldn't take a cut of any sales. If a font sold at all within the pay-what-you-want model, the designer would know they received every dollar. A lot of these choices were made to encourage an open and collaborative environment, and to keep things fun. Our initial launch had 10 fonts, and we've since grown to more than 50.

Lost Type was started on a dare, and it has gone on to become a successful model. Do you consider yourselves entrepreneurs?
I definitely consider myself to be an entrepreneur, and I know Tyler does as well. His involvement in Lost Type has diminished over time, as he has become more involved in his own startups. I think a lot of designers aspire to create something bigger than themselves. I get to work with shapes and colors all day — it's sort of like advanced preschool. I love my job,

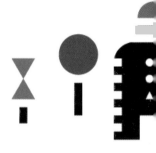

and I'm very passionate about it, but a feeling remains of wanting to do something bigger. I get to work with everyone from giant corporations to little mom-and-pop startups, and I get to experience the thrills of starting a business, vicariously. I was raised in small businesses, and it reminds me of growing up. But sometimes that thrill reaches a point that makes you want to start your own projects, such as Lost Type. The thrill and excitement at every step of the way has made Lost Type very rewarding in that sense.

Let's talk about the monetization of the site and the pay-what-you-want model.
Lost Type is a healthy marketplace, and everyone involved is very happy with the outcome. We've put the power in the hands of the customers, and they have been respectful and used it well. We will be making some interesting upgrades to the model, as time goes on, but so far it has been very rewarding.

During the first year or so, we've also sold T-shirts, button kits and printed specimen books through our store, and those offerings will be increasing very soon as well.

One of the most exciting things for us to watch is all of the instances of the fonts in use—do you have a favorite example?
I take a lot of pride in seeing the fonts go out into the world, and the examples we've seen of the fonts in use are always thrilling. Sometimes a font is submitted that is ready to release right away, but oftentimes I get to actually watch the designer's progress in creating it, and watch it

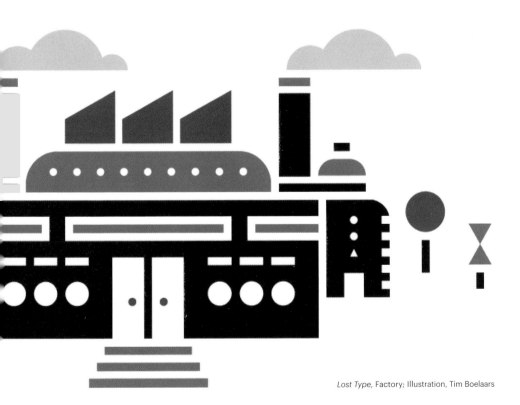

Lost Type, Factory; Illustration, Tim Boelaars

'grow up,' prior to release, which makes it even more thrilling to see it in use, for me. Seeing Obama use many of our fonts in his 2012 presidential campaign was very exciting. They used several of our fonts in his 'Dinner with Barack' campaign, as well as his campaigns in support of Hispanic and LGBT voters. At the same time, it's equally impactful to see small businesses using Lost Type. There is a certain philanthropic angle to the project as a whole. It has been a goal to increase the base standard of design quality in the world, and it's always nice to see us getting closer to that when a doughnut shop that could be using stretched type adopts one of our fonts instead.

Are you trained as a type designer, or is this a skill that you've picked up along the way?
After picking up those first few books, I became more interested and slowly taught myself to draw letters. I've picked up a few tricks here and there with the help of my friends in the field, and I've enjoyed employing those skills in my day-to-day work, in custom logotypes, for instance. I have several new fonts in the works that I'm looking forward to releasing.

Has the success of Lost Type benefited your practice or other font designers' practices, in terms of being 'known for something?'
We keep a 'company directory' on the site, with links to everyone who has contributed. That helps drive traffic to those people's portfolios and helps them to become known in the community. I've really enjoyed drawing attention to these wonderful designers, who have helped build Lost Type into what it is today.

Personally, it's hard to gauge how Lost Type has affected my career, but I'm sure it has been a positive influence. I've met a great deal of wonderful people during the course of the project, and many of them have since become my close friends. It has been great fun, and I assume it will continue to be so.

Are there influences outside of graphic design that have informed your practice?
Design seems to be running my life lately. I suppose it depends on how far removed from design you want to get. I'm very interested in history and specifically the history of the merger between industry and design. Working in branding, it's interesting for me to go back to the beginnings of that concept, historically, to Egyptian hieroglyphics, or Scottish tartans or the Industrial Revolution. Those are the beginnings of my trade, and it fascinates me to pour over old trademark books and think about the companies that they were associated with, lost to history but very important to the growth of that era.

Industrial design of the '30s to '60s inspires me a great deal. I'm a huge Raymond Loewy fan. He'd take a clunky, boxlike refrigerator and turn it into a streamlined beauty. Even in his day, that work was used as a case study for design and its applicability to mass-market products. I suppose it plays into the concept of 'doing something bigger.' I'm inspired by the work of the masters, such as Loewy and [Norman] Bel Geddes, and specifically how large their contribution to our culture has become, both in concept and execution.

Lost Type, Logo

Josh Brewer | Designer, Twitter | San Francisco, CA

52 WEEKS of UX

A discourse on the process of designing for real people.

The following posts have been tagged week 1

☞ WEEK 01

THE FIRST RULE OF UX

"You cannot not communicate. Every behaviou communication. Because behaviour does not h is no anti-behaviour), it is not possible not to (Watzlawick's First Axiom of Communication

This is the first rule of UX. Everything a design experience. From the purposeful addition of a (negligent omission of crucial messaging, every future of the people we design for.

As such, one of the primary goals of any good d the *intended* message...the one that leads to a (The copy-writing, the color of your text, the ali using all-caps or going lowercase on those navi absence of a design pattern—are all part of this

Knowing this, we can ask (and hopefully answe element support or contradict what I am trying user?" And by asking this you will find yourself the little things; the things that often go unsaid ultimately make up the user's experience.

JANUARY 6, 2010 *by* JOSHUA BREWER
TAGS: *communication watzlawick week 1*

52 Weeks of UX, Website Detail

"Right now more than ever, dialogue within the design community is essential."

Josh Brewer

Create to Share

Josh Brewer creates tools that benefit others. He started a blog, 52 Weeks of UX, with his partner, Josh Porter, that came out of their joint desire to share what he had learned. He freelanced, taught and ultimately decided that he wanted to do more with his UX skills than build brochure websites — so, he got involved in startups.

In all of the products that Josh helps shape — 52 Weeks of UX, Slacker Personal Radio, Socialcast and now, as a designer at Twitter — he creates products that are shared and products that build communities.

Can you give us a little bit about your background and how you made your way to Twitter?

I guess it would be back in high school, when I wanted to be an art teacher. However, I ended up graduating college with a history degree, moving to San Diego in 2000, and began teaching at a private elementary school. I started teaching kids how to use computers and soon realized that I was also teaching the teachers how to use them. It was eye-opening. I always look back to that experience as one of my very first moments of understanding the pain of using technology and why the user experience mattered.

I freelanced, taught and soon decided that I wanted to do more than build brochure websites, so I got involved with a few startups. I tried to take on as much as I could; I helped build products, worked with engineering teams, CEOs, the whole nine yards. I worked for a few startups — Slacker Personal Radio and SuggestionBox — but it was at Socialcast, a collaboration platform, that I realized the importance of engaging design at every point of a product's life cycle. I joined Socialcast at a very early stage, and I worked on everything. I worked shoulder-to-shoulder with the CEO to shape the product vision. I built with the engineers. I created the designs and wrote the front-end code. I slowly built up a team, helped to grow the company, and ended leaving to join Twitter six months before VMware ended up acquiring them.

I realized I was part of creating something that people found a lot of value in. I knew from talking to our customers the huge impact the service had on transforming their businesses. Socialcast was, in my opinion, one of the most successful things I've been a part of.

With all of the companies I've worked with, I realized that I love the challenge of figuring out a product. I love the iterative process—the ability to do as much up front research as you can, to talk to people, to figure out what's going on, to figure out the pain points, and to look at what you have—and then turn around, take all of that information, and turn it into something tangible. Then you can tell whether you've got it.

You cocreated 52 Weeks of UX to provide 'discourse on the process of designing for real people.' Can you talk about the idea and motivation for that site?

I learned most of my UX skills at the 'School of Hard Knocks.' I also read constantly and consider myself a lifelong learner. I think if you're in this business, you'd better really like to learn because the industry is changing at such an incredible pace. That's not to say that you have to be on top of everything, but you at least need to want to learn. 52 Weeks of UX came out of a desire to share the things I had learned. I partnered with my friend Josh Porter with a simple goal: to produce and share tangible, digestible lessons that people could walk away from every week and immediately apply to their jobs.

That project sparked off a really great relationship that Josh and I still have to this day. We constantly push each other to do more and share more. If 52 Weeks of UX had existed when I was just getting going, I would have devoured it. But it didn't, so we created it. The whole purpose of it really was to give back.

Are writing and dialogue important to your practice? Are they are important within the context of the design community?

I have two parts to my answer. One is that I think it is incredibly helpful to write. The process of putting your thoughts and ideas down on paper or on screen, thinking them through, and hitting publish—or save—is an incredible tool for self-reflection. It's hard. It's even harder to do it consistently. If you can get into a rhythm of writing, even in small increments, it's easy to keep it going. Find a simple tool that allows you to do that.

Right now more than ever, dialogue within the design community is essential. We are in such a new transition again, and it feels much like the early days of the web standards. This era of responsive web design that Ethan Marcotte kicked off is really just the tip of the iceberg. Whether people like to admit it, we have uncovered that the way we have been designing for the web does not actually, truly embrace the web. We add constraints like fixed widths because it's hard to figure out five different scenarios for how something should maintain relationships as it evolves. The reality is that in order to keep this thing moving forward, we need to write more, and we need to have conversations.

We need to be OK with saying, 'Here's an experiment that I did; I think it works,' and then find out a week later, that, no, actually it was crap, and that there is a much better way to do it.

You've talked about the end of the era of the rock-star designer, the emergence of teams, and the importance of who you choose to work with. How do you set up a framework for collaboration?

I really do think that era is kind of seeing its end. It will always kind of be there because humans are humans, but if you look at the way people are working, more people are teaming up. Right? They purposefully do projects with other people because it makes them better. It pushes them more. It puts them in a position where they have to think through, articulate and talk about solutions to these problems. There are many times when two brains are definitely better than one, even if it's just to have someone to bounce ideas off.

At Twitter, I spend a fair amount of time brainstorming and facilitating. Part of my job is to push, challenge, ask questions and point out places where we went right but could have gone left and ask, 'What would have happened then?' That's something that we do a lot and something that we encourage amongst the team at Twitter. Even if a specific task is assigned to someone, that designer will almost always talk through the idea with someone else. The way we've set up the teams drives that kind of communication. In a really healthy way, we end up with a lot more cross-pollination and integrated thinking across the company.

Along that same line, which kinds of designers thrive in a startup environment?
Someone who says, 'yes'—self-motivated designers and those who are willing to stretch and take on stuff that they might not normally do. You need an openness and ability to learn quickly because the reality is, in the startup world you're going to do 10 different things. That's just how it is. That kind of environment can be taxing, and you have to be vigilant and make sure that you keep a balance, but I also think it makes you a better designer. That constant need for agility stretches you in ways that you might not traditionally stretch yourself.

Is it relevant and important for designers to invest in learning about business, or is it just about finding the right partnerships?
I do think it's important. The day that I started sitting in on meetings with the CEO and talked about things such as conversion metrics and the lifetime of a customer as it relates to our product,

Twitter, Logo

it definitely changed the way I think about what I was working on and how I solve certain problems. I would love to see more business-minded designers. But that doesn't mean that designers need to do all of the business tasks, so that's where partnerships play a big role.

If you aren't business-minded, if you don't care about business, or if you aren't even aware that business is something you should care about, then you won't include that in part of your framework and your foundation for when you approach the problem you're trying to solve.

What are your thoughts on leadership — can it be taught? Does it need to be taught?
Leadership is super important. If a company has someone at the head of the ship, and he or she doesn't know what they're doing, but they have the 'title' of being in charge, it can be detrimental to the people who put their faith in that source of leadership. I think leadership is important. Period.

There will always be a need for some level of leadership in any business, because at the end of the day, someone is going to call the shots. For a designer thinking about leadership in a startup environment, some of the best leadership training is modeling. For example, when you are in a critique or a design review with designers, take note of the conversation and then relay what you've learned about how they handle situations by watching the interaction. You can then say, 'Hey, in this moment, you could've steered the conversation this way, and then you would have been able to keep it heading in the direction that you were looking for.' That's one tiny example.

In daily tasks, leadership comes with actually doing what you say you'll do. I know it's super cliché, but if you say you're going to do something and then you don't, your integrity comes into question. If you break your word enough times people lose faith and lose trust in your ability to actually lead them. Invariably

Twitter, iPhone Application

someone else will start leading, regardless of whether they have a title. In lot of ways, leadership comes from action, way more than it comes from prescribing rules and regulations.

What do you think the most exciting thing about the future of design is?
So, I'm not exactly sure that we know how to design for a distributed web. Design has traditionally had this awesome constraint of a page. A page has known, fixed elements — width and height — that the proportions, margins and grid are based on. Then the web came along.

Some people will tell you that the web was responsive from its beginning and that we were the ones who imposed a fixed width on it. I think that's true, but I think we did that because we definitely didn't have the tools in the beginning to even think differently, and approach building and designing things in a way that's responsive to the context, the device and the experience it is being created for. I hope that we continue to uncover and stumble upon ideas — such as responsive web design — that make us say, 'Oh, here's a new key that helps us think about the web.' Those are the ideas and moments that I am most excited about.

I am excited about the ability to design an experience, all the way from a feature phone, to an AppleTV, to everything in between. And to actually be able to create a system that works and retains its relationship and ratios and proportions and all that stuff. To me, that is crazy interesting and exciting. And it's not easy.

What advice would you give someone who has previously run a client-driven studio and wants to run a startup? Where are the resources for young designers?
There is just so much work out there. Period. Whether it's in client-services or a hybrid approach. I know a number of people who opened their own studio with one or two other people, started doing client work, and as soon

as they got a little bit of positive cash flow, they started pushing that toward a product idea they had. I've seen that over and over again, and I think that is super healthy. There are people out there doing everything they can to help designers make the transition into being a founder, a cofounder, or just to help them meet the right people who can advise them. The Designer Fund is one example.

That said — the Internet. Straight up. I could list half a dozen people off the top of my head who are 25 and younger who went from nowhere to being fairly well-known, and somewhat well-regarded, because they use the Internet correctly. It takes two steps: a) doing really good work, and b) knowing how to market yourself. And that happens all the time.

Twitter is pretty beneficial for that.
Indeed it is.

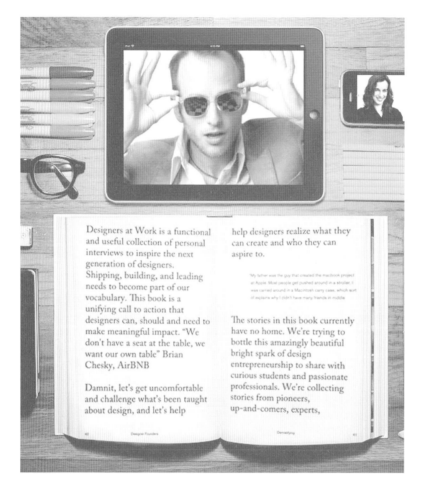

Designer Founders, Kickstarter Promotion

"Discovery and invention lie under conditions
of extreme uncertainty."

Enrique Allen

Learn by Doing

Enrique Allen always has been ahead of his time. He was tapped to attend Stanford's d.school when he was a freshman. He taught experimental courses at Stanford that created precursors to applications such as Path. He was a product developer at Venrock, a top-tier venture capital fund, and worked with startups such as AskMeGo, a live question-and-answer site, which according to Enrique might just have been ahead of the curve.

   Now, as cofounder of the Designer Fund, he's right on time. The Designer Fund provides angel funding, mentorship and network connections specifically for designers. Enrique encourages entrepreneurs to have a deep motivation and love for whom they serve and what they build.

Can you tell us a little bit about your background and how you found design?
My first design opportunities came unexpectedly when I created murals and a virtual tour for underserved communities as a freshman at Stanford University. This service helped me realize that stories can and should last for generations in both the digital and physical environment. I became interested in the power of technology to intentionally influence how we live while doing research in the Persuasive Tech Lab and helped produce work such as Peace on Facebook. This work opened my eyes to the potential to change people's behavior on a massive scale with something as simple as a virtual hug or status update. I was invited to be a designer inside a venture capital fund called Venrock with a few of their startups before graduate school. I began to learn more about education as a teaching assistant at Stanford's d.school, where I taught courses ranging from data mining, persuasive video, iPhone mapping and cross-culture design to digital media design. I became passionate about proving that design can make an impact in the context of early-stage startups.

   When I got the opportunity to help run Facebook's fbFund—a Y Combinator-like experiment with 20-plus companies building on the Facebook platform or using Facebook Connect—it was a great chance to directly apply methods from the d.school. Although I had never run an accelerator, I was hands-on in everything from the selection, space design and mentor network to the curriculum, which culminated in Demo Day. I also ran a small design team that did short sprints with companies to help with new user experiences. Long story short, multiple companies were acquired, and more than half received additional rounds of funding. Many of these startups are doing well to this day, such as Samasource, Life360, Zimride, TaskRabbit and Wildfire. FbFund turned into a successful proof of concept which then informed the thesis of 500 Startups, which I was invited to help start as I finished graduate school.

500 Startups was like fbFund all over again, except we started from scratch, and it was 10 times harder. Craig Mod and I worked on the brand and early website iterations, and I spent the first few months redesigning the space in downtown Mountain View, Calif. Designing and building out the space was a big lesson in how space can provide a context for creative behavior. I selected and worked with more than 50 startups for our accelerator program while I created a framework for our operations. I woke up every day thinking about how I could provide scalable design resources. I experimented with a number of ways for designers to engage with our companies, ranging from office hours, talks, workshops, design reviews to community events such as the Product Design Guild.

It's been so rewarding to see startups practice design techniques and apply lessons on their own. We've had multiple acquisitions, and many of our accelerator companies have started to grow and hire full-time designers in-house. After working to instill design thinking in three, then 20, then hundreds of startups, my questions started to shift toward how to make great design part of the DNA of startups and have a longer-term impact.

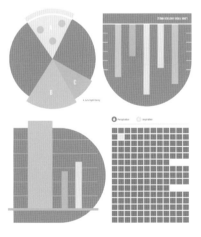

Designer Founders, Lettering; Design, Matt Stevens

Instead of asking how I can help startups design better products, I ask, 'How might I help startups help themselves design better products?'

Can you describe The Designer Fund and your motivation for starting it?

The Designer Fund began in the spring of 2011 in partnership with 500 Startups, Khosla Ventures, Kleiner Perkins, Andreessen Horowitz and other top early-stage investors. We provide angel funding, mentorship and network connections to designers. To date, we've invested in 10 companies, some of which are graduates of top accelerators such as Y Combinator. We produce public-facing research, such as our infographic and the *Designer Founders* book, as well as events such as The Designer Fair. The Designer Fund is a vehicle that creates a virtuous positive-feedback loop for successful designers to give back to the next generation of aspiring entrepreneurial designers. Our mission is to create the best community of designers, whose success in business generates positive social impact. We look for startups that not only have technical but also, specifically, design talent in their DNA. After leading design-thinking exercises with startups in the portfolios of Facebook Fund and 500 Startups, I realized that strong design leadership at the founding-team level is critical to an integrated and sustained culture of design. You can host design workshops, office hours and consult, which are all helpful, but often startups revert back to their existing habits, and design becomes an add on, like putting lipstick on a pig. Who is going to lead, model and inspire design behaviors in everyone at a company? Who is going to truly champion the user-experience with the authority to make decisions?

We believe more designers can create startups with meaningful, positive social impact. We're building a bridge to help designers cross over to the startup world and align resources from angel money to big VCs. On a more personal note, I became a bit frustrated and jaded by startups that seemed to solve problems around superfluous and 'cool' factors with near-sighted outcomes. I've been lucky to travel a bit around the world and work on products for the other 90 percent with extreme.stanford.edu in emerging markets such as Myanmar and South Africa, which has helped me put things in perspective. I've seen too many talented people in Silicon Valley work on products that are incremental or not that life changing for anyone. By using the term 'designer,' we have a responsibility, even a moral obligation, to intentionally impact people's lives, hopefully for the better. Unfortunately, the products we design often waste people's valuable resources and their attention, which is more scarce than money and time. Why is it that there are so many talented people working on shallow problems?

The deeper I got into venture capital, I noticed a fundamental feedback loop between talent, capital and liquidity. Venture capitalists invest in creating the future state of things, but ultimately they're accountable to their partners, who range from university endowments and pension funds, to oil companies. Those are the faceless institutions that expect a large financial return and can be indifferent to the product sold — whether it's sugar water or a product that saves babies — as long as it makes money. These partners shape innovation and put pressure on many U.S.-based investors to have a 'home-run' mentality, so naturally, VCs look for startups with the potential for big returns through acquisitions and IPOs. But here lies the chicken-and-egg problem.

Many investors are philosophically interested in opportunities such as education and emerging markets, but there aren't many examples of successful startups in those areas, so how can they justify making those bets to their partners? For example, if a VC invests millions into a photo-sharing startup that is eventually acquired by a well-known platform company, thus creating wealth and fame all over TechCrunch, that recognition sends a direct signal back to aspiring entrepreneurs and talented students to also create photo apps. Unfortunately that cycle doesn't encourage young designers to create, say, alternative energy products in East Africa. Luckily it doesn't have to be this way.

The emergence of crowdfunding and initiatives such as the JOBS act will help fuel new system-level changes. Hopefully, as a community, we can back businesses whose core economic engine inherently creates positive social impact and improves our environment.

How did the *Designer Founders* book start? What is it about demystifying entrepreneurs' stories that is important to share?
We think it's really important to highlight the paths of emerging to established entrepreneurial designers, so that young designers can be inspired to believe and act. 'I can,' and 'Just do it,' pretty much sum it up.

We hope to show the particulars of how some designers have evolved from self-taught to traditionally trained backgrounds, and hopefully readers can recognize insights in their own lives. One of our core values is giving back, so every year we'll create educational resources such as this book for the design community, especially for young design students worldwide.

At the end of the day, we practice what we preach by going out into the field and learning from these people. It's especially important if we want to foster a great community and invest in the next generation of successful designers.

How have you seen the startup environment shift in a way that has opened the door for designers to become founders?
We're building on the shoulders of giants who've fought for decades. I was rereading Bill Buxton's, *Sketching User Experiences: Getting the Design Right and the Right Design*. He makes a case for the importance of design by outlining Apple's trajectory. As I was reading this, I was reminded that we're doing nothing new — we're just carrying on a legacy and evolving it. Apple of course is an easy example for me to cite because it works. For people to perceive a new or unknown product as valuable, it likely needs to meet the status quo and then exceed expectations. With Apple's financials, people can compare it against all other companies and clearly see how Apple is outperforming them with fundamentally better design in so many dimensions of their business.

Like with any paradigm shift, it takes years for something to cross the chasm, and startups are realizing that partnering with a designer early on can be a great thing. Adapting Wilson Miner's quote (pg 72), designers are not only being invited to sit at the table, they are now offered the opportunity to own the table — if they can step up to help build it. No more excuses; the impact will speak for itself.

What avenues are available for designers who are fluent in well-crafted design and have entrepreneurial ambitions but are unfamiliar with the business side?
There are so many avenues and DIY resources emerging that I can barely keep up. Nearly every top school has entrepreneurial courses, and alternative forms of education — such as General Assembly's curriculum — are sprouting up in different permutations. To paraphrase Mike Krieger, the cofounder of Instagram, 'One day on the job as a real entrepreneur is worth more than all the entrepreneurship books combined.' I think young designers can easily grow into the business side of things and just learn it by doing it.

Just recognize when you need help, and don't be afraid to ask. It's that simple.

SCOTT BELSKY
& MATIAS COREA

BEHANCE

Scott Belsky was working in the leadership development team at Goldman Sachs when he approached Matias Corea in 2005 with the idea for Behance, an online platform for creatives to showcase their work. Scott was looking for a partner who understood design and the creative process to help build Behance, and Matias was a print and brand designer who had never designed a website before. Launched in 2008, they built a profitable business with over a million users before taking VC funding. They have grown to include the 99U conference and Action Method, a task-management product line.

Designer Founders, Digital Book

What would you say to a designer who works in the client-service world to get them to think about working for a startup?

Pick up side projects that will help you form a strong team, make sure that you're passionate, and build a skill set that's valuable in a startup. Consulting can train you to be a better consultant, likewise, working in a startup will help you become a better startup designer. There were many designers working with startups during the first Internet bubble, and many of them got burned. It's OK for designers to tiptoe in and see that not all that glitters is gold, but eventually they need to commit full throttle and be comfortable being uncomfortable. Discovery and invention lie under conditions of extreme uncertainty, and in spaces and problems that seem frighteningly ambitious.

Do you have advice for designers who want to follow their passion and be entrepreneurs?

Join a startup, and cut your teeth a bit. The world doesn't need another amateur rock band. Focus on forming the best team above all else—it's the one variable you can control. Have a deep motivation of love for whom you're serving and what you're building. Ask yourself five 'why' questions—if the answers end in some version of fame, money or power, start over again.

What are some of the key attributes or personality traits of designer founders?

The designer founders that we have observed are consistently multidisciplinary and have the cross-functional skills necessary to make product decisions. They are fluent in the full design stack, ranging from user research, product design, interaction design, information architecture and graphic design to communication design. They might not be experts in all subdisciplines of design but can get by on their own in the early days of their startup and attract specialists when needed. In addition, they have a thorough enough working understanding of technology and business stacks, including agile programming and data-based marketing methods. Designer founders can move up and down the design stack and horizontally through the technology and business stacks to do what it takes to ship and use data to justify their decisions when needed. Thus, they are capable of leading both their product and organization through the design cycles needed to innovate. There is a difference between a designer who can design a dashboard in a car and a designer who can design a whole car and then learn how to drive it. Designer founders need to be able to do both, but don't confuse cofounder with CEO. Designers can still be founders without being CEOs.

As much as I love many of the things that Steve Jobs embodied, I'd love to invest in more of the Jony Ive's of the world—more of the product designers behind the scenes.

Designer Fund, Website

Jake Nickell | Cofounder, Threadless | Chicago, IL

Stay Free Forever, T-shirt; Illustration, Jeremyville

"I think the most important thing we can do is try to encourage curiosity, encourage a desire to figure out how things work, and contribute."

Jake Nickell

Make Work With Friends

Jake Nickell got hooked on the Internet and started a culture of makers. He founded Threadless, an online community of artists and e-commerce store in 2000 — years before terms such as "user innovation," "crowdsourcing" and "open source" were in regular circulation in the business and technology worlds.

Threadless generates ideas for new T-shirts by asking their customers to submit designs and then vote on them. Customers tell the company exactly what shirts they want to buy, so products sell out. Jake created a genius recipe for success — one that looks at the designer as both the creator and the consumer.

What is your background, and how did you come to design?

I've always enjoyed drawing. In high school I did a fair amount of graffiti. I was always carrying a black book with me, sketching in it constantly. When I first got the Internet in '95, I taught myself how to build a website and built a site for all of my drawings. That's when I really got into web design. When the time came to figure out what to do about college, I was split between going into computer engineering and web design. I decided to go to art school for multimedia and web design. At that time I also got invited to this amazing little design forum called Dreamless.org—that's when it really started getting serious for me. It was a weird time with all these little design portals made by super-talented designers around the world who were playing with the Internet. Surfstation, K10k, kiiroi.nu, h73—all these amazing little corners of the web—I was hooked.

What are your thoughts looking back on how Threadless has grown from a desire to make things with your friends into one of the largest crowdsourced design communities in the world?

I think part of our success can be attributed to a greater cultural movement that I'm stoked about. When I was in high school, everyone wore T-shirts with big companies' logos. We all listened to the same music, and we all watched the same three TV shows. Now, there is so much more individuality. I'm really glad that we're moving away from a mass-produced culture to one that's more about what makes us all unique. When I started Threadless, I didn't think it could ever be anything big because I didn't think there were enough people in the world who would care. The Internet has made the world a much smaller, more connected place.

Have you been a part of other successful side projects?
A project I'm really excited about right now is called Nightmare Development. It's run by a group of snowboarders in Summit County, Colo., one who used to be a Threadless employee. They are building snowboards from scratch. I really like seeing people with the drive and determination to make things because they want to. It's so pure what these guys are doing. They have no other agenda but to simply make the best snowboard that they possibly can, have fun doing it, and share that with as many people who want to be a part of it.

When did you realize Threadless was more than a side project?
It took four years. The first two years I was working a full-time job and shipping orders on my lunch break. The next two years, I quit my job to start a web consultancy business and built websites for clients. Threadless was a side project — proof we knew how to build an e-commerce site. In 2004, we looked at the previous year and noticed we were making just as much money from Threadless sales as we were building websites.

So we fired all of our clients and started focusing on our own projects. Even then, we ended up creating a bunch of other new little projects. It wasn't until 2008 — eight years in — when we finally focused 100 percent of our energy on Threadless.

Do you see a resurgence of makers today, and how should we encourage consumer culture to become a culture of makers?
I don't have any data to back it up, but my gut says things are only getting better. There are so many great venues for people to do things with the things they make. Etsy, Kickstarter, YouTube — there are so many platforms where you can share, sell and discuss your creations with others — and they are working so well. Today, it's so easy to figure out how to make something. Twenty years ago, if I wanted to learn how to bake a perfect muffin, I would have had to go to the library and find a muffin cookbook. Now, I can pull out my phone and get access to a million recipes and step-by-step video instructions. The problem with all of this information is that it's easy to get caught up in being a passive viewer of it all. I think the most important thing we can do is try to encourage curiosity, encourage a desire to figure out how things work, and contribute.

You taught yourself web design; did you also teach yourself how to run a business?
Yes, pretty much anything I am decently skilled at was self-taught, or I learned it through

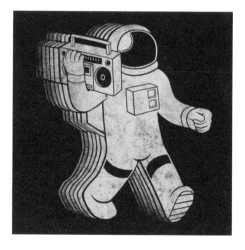

Funkalicious, T-shirt; Illustration, Christopher Golebiowski

experience. I don't feel like I'm the most business-savvy person in the world in the traditional sense. I love the business side of creating a product that people connect with, but I'm not as much into the other very important bits of running a business, such as financial stuff, legal stuff, HR stuff, etc.

Do you consider yourself an entrepreneur?
I do consider myself an entrepreneur, but I'm really glad the business is at the scale now where I can lean on other people who are really great at the stuff that I'm not.

How important is the culture of Threadless to the success and growth of the company?
The most important thing for me to maintain culture-wise is that everyone in the company knows why we are doing what we are doing, and that mission itself motivates them to work really hard to make it happen. You don't want people just there to collect a paycheck or working out of fear. As a company grows, it's harder to keep that mission top of mind for everyone. In addition to the culture a clear, shared mission provides, we do all kinds of other things to make working at Threadless fun. Our office environment is ridiculous. We have a huge atrium that's open to the public and where we host all kinds of events, from monthly free yoga classes, to bad '80s movie nights, to CreativeMornings' events.

Are you still hands-on as a designer?
Yes, but not really in any meaningful sense. I work very close with our creative team on our site design, copy, branding and products, but I'm not the one actually doing the work 99 percent of the time. I'd love to make time to do more.

What is the biggest risk you've taken?
Probably climbing Longs Peak in Colorado — that was insane. At Threadless I think the biggest risk was really early on when

I quit my job to pursue doing my own thing. It was still extremely small at that time, and it easily could have not worked out — it was the best decision I ever made.

What is your favorite failure?
I love it when you can turn a failure around to be a success for everyone. Like when a cease-and-desist letter is turned into a partnership or a ripped-off design into a collection of products by the original artist.

Do you have advice for designers who have entrepreneurial ambitions but are hesitant to take the risk to pursue them?
Stop hesitating. Start small, test it out, and let it build slowly over time. Have confidence in yourself to figure things out along the way.

What makes online business better for Threadless than the retail environment?
Our store started as an experiment to see what we could do in retail other than just hanging shirts on a rack. We were getting a ton of interest from stores that wanted to carry our products and were weary because it's so difficult to properly tell the story of how the T's came to be in-store.

The story is why we exist — it's what's most compelling about our products. Ideally, our knowledge would be applied to the way we work with partners to distribute our products, so they can be properly merchandised in-store.

Is the future of design entrepreneurship on the web, or are there opportunities for tangible goods to disrupt markets?
I definitely think the future of design entrepreneurship is not limited to the web. There are all kinds of disruption happening with tangible goods. Quirky is a great example, the site itself is a web-based platform, but I would argue that the inventors represented on the site are entrepreneurs in their own right.

Is the current technological landscape making more people open to collaboration? Should we all make things with our friends and hope they turn into careers?

I think the current technological landscape makes it really easy to find like-minded people to make things with. There are so many places you can go to collaborate with people on things you are interested in. For designers, dribbble is a great place to try making things with people. And yes, I think we should all always have side projects through which we make things with friends. It's so important to have a personal project, and you don't have to do it alone. You never know what'll happen.

Should we encourage designers to publish before their products are perfect?

It's not necessarily that you have to publish it right after you take the first step — it's more about getting things out of your head and onto the screen or paper. You can sit down and write a really great sentence or paragraph without having the next great American novel written in your head. I think many people don't even start because they are too busy trying to think out every angle and put together the perfect plan. That said, I do also think it's great to publish small pieces of finished work along the way wherever you possibly can before waiting for everything to be done and perfect — that'll never happen.

I started Threadless one hour after I came up with the idea by simply starting a thread on a forum, asking people to post designs to it and promising to print the best ones.

Threadless, Headquarters; Photo, Daniel Kelleghan

Katie Kirk | Cofounder, Eight Hour Day | Minneapolis, MN

Eli No!, Illustration Detail

"Remember, there is more to life than work."

Katie Kirk

Design Your Life

Eight Hour Day (EHD) was cofounded by Katie Kirk and Nathan Strandberg, a husband-and-wife design and illustration team. They have created a lifestyle in which work, life and inspiration all are equal.

They have produced award-winning work for clients such as Target, The New York Times *and the Walker Art Center, and have taken time to explore side projects that are as fulfilling as they are fun. They took a cross-country trip, working from city to city and sharing their experiences on their blog, and they have published an illustrated children's book,* Eli, No!

They remind themselves that there's more to life than work, and in doing so, have charted their own path to success.

Can you give us a bit of background on how you found each other, found design and found the passion to design a lifestyle for yourselves?

Yes, we actually met in design school at the University of Minnesota, Twin Cities, although we didn't start dating until a couple years later. When we did, it was pretty obvious that our love for creativity and design was a large part of our relationship and why it worked. It finally clicked everything else into place.

The fact that I get to be married to and work next to my best friend every day is pretty damn amazing. It has definitely let us define our lives in ways I never thought possible.

Eli, No! is a self-initiated project in which the storyline and characters came out of your personal lives. Can you talk a bit more about the decision to make _Eli, No!_? How did you find time to make the book?

Yes, the book was 100 percent inspired by our own chocolate lab, Eli. But the muse for the project was actually our nephew, Parker. Whenever he would come to visit, I would be trying to wrangle Eli and saying, 'Eli, no!'—and every time I said it, he would say it, too! He liked how fun it was to say.

I just thought, 'What a great idea for a book, a great refrain for kids to interact with. What kid doesn't love to yell no?'

Finding time for personal projects can be very difficult. This one was made at night, usually between the hours of 7 p.m. and 10 p.m over the course of a couple months. It's always a struggle when it comes to personal work for us. We are always trying to find the balance between work, personal projects and a life. So many ideas, so little time.

Do you consider yourselves entrepreneurs?
No, not yet, but we're working on it.

Are there more self-initiated products and applications in Eight Hour Day's future?
Definitely. Most of our personal projects are ones that we feel can expand the business in some way—not only from a growth standpoint, but also creatively as well.

What is it like to have complete creative control over a project?
Glorious. Nerve-wracking. Some of the best projects are the ones you do for yourself. Some of the most frustrating projects are the ones you do for yourself.

Your trip across the country looked incredibly inspirational and fun. What was the motivation to take the adventure? When did you finally decide it was time to do it?
Originally, we were going to move to San Francisco, however, when we started looking at rent costs, we realized that we could, for the same cost, get vacation rentals across the U.S. for a year. As soon as we figured that out, we both knew that was what we were going to do. I think we felt restless. I think we were looking for an adventure. I think we were looking to answer a lot of questions we had rolling around.

We imagine meeting your peers in person was a welcome difference from the Twitter chatter. How do you use the Internet to build your brand?

It's so amazing to meet many of these people in person. I feel truly blessed to be in a profession filled with so many fantastic individuals. I think we are out there in the typical ways: through our blog, Twitter, Pinterest, etc. Our biggest thing is that we try to build our personal site in a way that helps us put new work up easily, to try to keep things current. We also try to rebrand every couple of years as well.

How do you think your journey will change the future of your design practice?
I think we are just really excited to be settled and put in a full 100 percent on the business again, which was difficult at times on the trip. I think we're excited to have that time to focus again—I don't think we'll take it for granted ever again.

You have a wonderful blog that is as much about your lives as creatives as is it beautiful design work, and you also are a husband and wife working together. How important is it to share your lives with the design community and present an authentic view into your world?
Obviously, like most blogs, it's probably not fully authentic—it's not showing everything, like the little bickering that's happening over a concept or who should take out the trash—but all and all, it's pretty honest view of things that inspire us. The blog was very new to us before creating it for the trip, but it's so great to have a running journal of what happened, whom you met and what you're into at that time. We find ourselves going back through the pages a lot.

What is the biggest risk you have taken to build Eight Hour Day?
The biggest risk was just starting the studio and fully committing.

What is your favorite failure?
Our favorite failure was getting let go as an interactive vendor for Target in 2008. At the

time, they changed their interactive-vendor policy from working with a number of smaller independent shops to working with a small handful of agencies. We were one of a lot of places let go that day. It was less than a week before we were going to take our very first remote working trip to San Francisco. At first we were pretty bummed. The day we found out we just went home and started drinking on the porch. However, once we finally made it out to San Francisco, we really used the time to focus on the business, restrategize and rebrand. We went out searching for inspiration around the city and the Alameda flea market. We both agree it was one of our favorite projects we've worked on together.

Do you have advice for designers who want to follow their passions to design a life they love?
Neither of us is the biggest risk taker, but we work really hard trying to make our dreams a reality. Start small, and set aside time to create the things you want. Save money. Meet people. Get your work out there as much as you can. Focus on creating things that excite you. Always try to get better, and try new things. Remember, there is more to life than work.

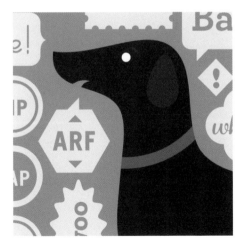

Eli No!, Illustration Detail

Great Gatsby Business Card, Letterpress Print Detail

"We get restless. And I think that's where
that entrepreneurial spirit comes from."

Dusty Summers

Stay Restless

Dusty Summers and Jason Kernevich are the duo behind The Heads of State, a graphic design and illustration studio based in Philadelphia. Their brilliantly simplistic and conceptual image making has made the pair favorites of the editorial illustration scene. Their latest self-initiated venture, Pilot & Captain, a collection of city-specific T-shirts and posters, is an extension of their Travel Series prints.

Dusty and Jason developed the Travel Series into a successful print series and now into an expanding product company. They've simply built upon their passions — whether travel, T-shirts or tattoos — and they've created side projects that last around themes that they love.

How did you discover design, and how did your collaboration begin?
We both graduated from Tyler School of Art in 2001. Our collaboration really grew out of a desire to stay creative after work. We started designing posters for shows we'd go see, and that snowballed into a full-fledged design studio over the last eight years or so.

What do you each bring to the collaboration? How do you handle overlaps in your skill sets?
Having worked together for so long, we've got a little bit of shorthand down. There were a number of years where we worked on separate coasts, and our collaboration happened over the phone or on instant message. That sort of long-distance collaboration forces you to be brief and to the point when pitching or explaining a concept. Now that we're together in an office, that basis has only served to help in the collaboration. There's an inherent trust that lets us be a little more outspoken toward each other than we normally would be. With eight years of history behind us, it makes it OK to say, 'That's a terrible idea,' or, 'Start over. That looks like total garbage.'

Do you consider yourselves entrepreneurs?
We get restless. And I think that's where that entrepreneurial spirit comes from. We've gone from poster designers to illustrators to designers,

and that need to continue to branch out always seems to creep up.

In addition to your editorial and poster illustration work, do you have a strategy for pushing self-initiated work?

You've got to make time. Whether that means saying no to client work or putting in extra hours in the evening. Over the last year, we've seen some success with these self-initiated pieces — such as the Travel Series posters and now Pilot & Caption — and we've realized that these types of projects can be a cornerstone to a business strategy. We've made it policy to each set aside one week for one partner to do whatever they want. Whether that's laying the basis for a self-initiated project or learning a new technique or focusing on promotional material. It's important, and it's hard to stick to because when a client is calling, you've got to make that mature decision. If you continue to be creative and allow yourself time, then the client work will continue to roll in. But if you get stagnant, that will dry up very quickly.

Can you tell us a bit about how the Travel Series posters came to be?

My wife and I have a small collection of 1950s and '60s travel posters — pieces by Nathan Garamond, David Klein and others — and this is what I see every day when I get home. As much as there is a style associated with our work, Jason and I really believe that the root of our work is concept based, and often we don't get a chance to explore something solely stylistically. The travel posters gave us an opportunity to go

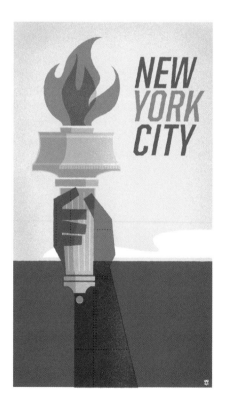

Travel Series Posters, Various Cities

for something that we don't get to do. It started as a project for *Real Simple* magazine as a series of 1-inch spot illustrations for, 'The Most Livable Cities.' We accepted the job with terms that we would just have fun doing these inspired travel pieces. We then went back and built them out for a full series of posters.

Do you have plans for more work outside of your client responsibilities?
We have too many plans—that seems to always be the problem. We've definitely got some extension of the Travel Series posters series landing soon, moving into more of an apparel approach for it. And we've got a number of illustration and type series ideas we're constantly working on, just have to see which makes it to the finish line first.

You've taken some of your client-based illustrations out of their original context and sold them as art prints. Do you often think about different ways to monetize the work?

No, it's not until after, when we can identify some pieces that have a life beyond what they're intended for. I think that speaks to the simplicity of our illustrations. Often an image that was done for a client's annual report looks just as good on a bedroom wall as it does next to some financial analysis. We've tried in the past to just produce work as art prints, and we quickly realized we weren't artists; we need a goal, a problem to solve in order to be inspired by the piece. Just sitting down and making fun images isn't, for the most part, that exciting for us.

What is your favorite project?

We've got a soft spot for an early poster we did for Wilco. It's simple, just a vine wrapping around the Washington Monument. This was the first time we found the opportunity to bring a little social commentary to our work. It really marks the point where we fell out of love with gig posters and in love with illustration, specifically making images that send a message or solve a problem.

What is your favorite failure?

Like any designer or illustrator, there have been any number of missed opportunities. We get upset, first at the client and then with ourselves. We've got to keep reminding ourselves that at the end of the day, we're in a service industry; someone is hiring us to give him or her something. And if they're not happy, we should figure out how to fix that. When the project goes south, there's always a meeting over beers to say, 'Let's put egos aside. We could have done this and this to make it better.'

We did a solo gallery show, and while it was well attended, man, we just didn't enjoy the process. Again, there was no goal, and yes, we could have set our own parameters, but for us,

the whole thing felt a little hollow, just making pieces to be hung on the walls. It was an amazing opportunity. Next time we'll need to get ourselves into the right frame of mind.

Do you have any advice for designers with entrepreneurial ambitions?

As a designer, you always bitch and moan over let's say an accountant who hires his brother to do a half-assed logo for him. Don't make that same mistake. You're good, great, at making imagery. Find someone who is great at balancing your books. Find someone who is great at programming. There are going to be things that you want to handle, things that you've got an interest in, but for everything else, the time and trouble isn't worth the money you think you're saving.

What interests outside of design have most influenced your practice?

The ability to just unplug in a movie theater or on the couch with a book is one of our biggest influences. Movies and books expose you to

Pilot & Captain, New York Airports

someone else's view of the world, some strange tweaked aspect or angle that you might never experience except through this outlet. Having kids has been a big influence as well. Kids allow you to get on the carpet and get your hands dirty with Legos or see a stick turn into a rocket launcher. There's a lot to be learned.

Do your speaking engagements change the way you think about your work and what value you're adding to the world?
Most definitely. Though we love speaking, the most gratification comes from lectures at colleges. We can give these kids an idea of what they can do, and that their 'job' doesn't have to be an office job. We can tell them they can set their own terms, and with a little bit of tenacity, they can chart their own course. I think it's also a great venue to tell folks what we've learned. We can try to convince them that common knowledge isn't exactly correct, that you don't need a mega account to keep a studio afloat and live a comfortable life, that design doesn't have to start and end with clients.

Scott Wilson | Founder, MINIMAL (MNML) | Chicago, IL

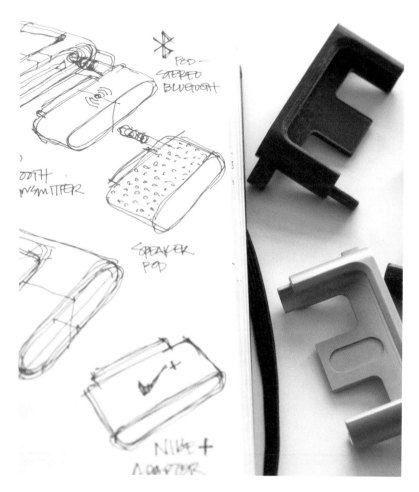

TikTok+LunaTik, Sketches and Parts

"You have to have courage, and you have to be fearless."

Scott Wilson

Make Your Ideas Real

Scott Wilson is a designer, serial entrepreneur and all around game-changer. He is the former Global Creative Director of Nike, has led design organizations such as IDEO, Thomson Consumer Electronics, Fortune Brands and Motorola, and has jumped from job to job, leaving when he felt it was time to learn more.

He founded his studio MINIMAL (MNML) and evenly balances the practice between fee-based work and startup ventures. He often takes risks on ideas that others wouldn't, and his TikTok+LunaTik Multi-Touch Kickstarter campaign did just that. He challenged the idea of how great products get made and changed the way the world thinks about crowdfunding. He has paved the way for others to dream big and make their ideas real.

Can you tell us a little bit about your background?

My dad was an industrial designer and is a studied architect. As a kid, I found inspiration in the design books and magazines laying around the house. My first 'big kid' book was, *Rapid Viz: A New Method for the Rapid Visualization of Ideas*, a book that encourages you to get your ideas on paper and communicate them in sketch format — it's still a great resource today. I was constantly drawing in school, and I also liked physics, math and art. It is a good thing my dad was an industrial designer because my guidance counselors and teachers didn't know anything about design. I've pretty much always known that I wanted to be in the design world. Along the way, I've been a part of five startups, four corporations and three consultancies, and it has been a variety of back-and-forth on all sides of the fence. This range of experience has given me a wide, broad scope and visibility across how things work.

Did you set out to take an entrepreneurial route, or did it happen along the way?

I think it just happened naturally. In the beginning I learned the basics and the fundamentals. At my first consultancy, they didn't have any design — I was thrown into the fire and was client-phasing from the beginning, which was great. At my second job, I worked for Thomson Consumer Electronics. Philippe Starck, who was just in the beginning of his career, was our creative director, and I didn't even know who Starck was. You just fall into these kinds of things.

Do you consider yourself an entrepreneur?
In the early days, I jumped from job to job, and I always made the decision to move on when I felt like I needed to learn more. After five startups, maybe going on eight within the next year, I am an entrepreneur. My wife is not as excited about the startups and the nonpaying work as I am, but she trusts me.

What has drawn you to go out on your own?
I first got hooked on being part of an end-to-end experience at Nike, where they allowed me to drive as much of the process as I wanted. I dove in headfirst, and it's hard to go back to being confined to one particular part of design after that. There are many examples of companies that champion creative vision. Companies where the design-minded people sit at the table with all the decision makers. Apple is an obvious one.

But so many companies and clients still don't empower you to be involved in all the touch points along the way, and in the end, it's almost easier to just do it yourself. I guess that's why I'm drawn to a lot of startups.

Do new resources and tools such as Kickstarter empower designers to start their own projects and reach all touchpoints?
Tools such as Kickstarter are great for young designers or entrepreneurs who want to try their hand at starting a startup.

One of the most rewarding things about the TikTok+LunaTik Multi-Touch Kickstarter project was the inspiration it brought to a lot of people. But the success of that project was also based on my ability to draw from 20 years of

Nike Presto, Digital Bracelet

training and experience, which made it a little easier on the back end. A lot of people are finding out that it's a lot harder than you think.

How have you seen design's role change in startups over the years?

It's obvious that design is very important today. It's funny in retrospect because I think it has always been important. But the battle and the conversations happening today are different than they were five or even 10 years ago. Now everyone knows they need design. Whether they know what that means is the whole question. Only a few really get it.

Successful companies have fully invested in design. They've invested in the product, the packaging and the overall experience.

Look at a company such as Beats by Dr. Dre, which commands around 55 percent of the headphone market. They know their audience.

Look at a product such as Nest. Tony Fadell, who trained at Apple and founded the iPod, turned to Fred Bould, and together they created Nest. They saw an object—the thermostat—that nobody gave a crap about, and now all of a sudden, everybody wants it. There are other companies that get it—the formula is not a secret anymore—but for some reason, a lot of companies are scared to truly empower design at the decision-making level. It's obvious that the ones that do this have success because of the design and consistency, and the confidence that comes along with the messaging and storytelling.

Design's role has changed for the better. We owe a lot to Apple for leading the way and showing that design and good business go hand-in-hand.

With the understanding that design and business go hand-in-hand, and the idea that it's good for designers to be thrown into the startup world because they'll get some of the startup knowledge, how important is it for designers to be educated in business?

Formal training is nice, but I think you can definitely pick it up along the way. I did, but that was 20 years of learning—it's better if you can pick it up sooner rather than later. Business is part of the formula. It is part of what empowers and gives designers respect and part of what allows them to reach the decision-making level.

Business factors are sometimes things that are unrelated to the user, to the look and feel, or to the technology. But they all have realities in the marketplace with channels and buyers, and these channels are the gateway to the consumer.

If you do the right thing for the consumer, but you can't get to the consumer, then that's a problem. Digital tools, and consumer access through products such as Kickstarter, are making the consumers go out and seek the product versus taking all the power away from the buyer.

As a designer, you are a generalist. You take information from different disciplines to juggle and balance the recipe. You are more like a chef. One hundred percent of every ingredient doesn't make a good dish; you have to measure the ingredients to make the recipe delicious.

It is really important to understand the ingredients—both business and design—that make up a great product.

You talked a little about the shifting relationship between the consumer and the product. How has the digital fabrication revolution changed the way you think about the consumer process?

It's a fantastic new development. As a designer I think we all get addicted to the instant visual and functional gratification that comes from these new tools. No matter how well you visualize, until you see that first hyper-real rendering of the product or the prototype, it's just an idea—it sits around, and it gestates in your head, but it doesn't become tangible until you make it real. Then you can learn from it and refine it. One of the things that I learned at

Nike is that talk is cheap. People don't get an idea until you show them a physical product; that's when momentum builds.

IDEO's Tom Hulme said, 'Talk - Action = Shit.' I don't know how many times I've sat in meetings where people just talk, talk, talk and show renderings that just don't sell the idea until they put this physical thing on the table. Today's tools allow you to do that and do it fast. The TikTok+LunaTik was a great example. I was teaching myself SolidWorks, and I thought the watches would be a good project to test out the software. It was just a pet project. I thought, 'Maybe I'll make a prototype of this,' and $200 dollars later, I had my prototype. Then I thought, 'Oh, maybe people other than myself would like this.' I started showing it around, and everyone said, 'No it's too expensive, it's gotta be plastic, and it's gotta be cheap.' And I said no. In the end, I put it up on Kickstarter and saw what people really thought. The whole design process was honestly only a couple weeks' worth of work, $200 dollars and a Sunday to make a video. It was just me, working on it on the side, and people thought I was wasting my time.

How do you balance pet projects, whether they turn into leading projects or not, with your client work? Is it just a case-by-case decision, or do you have a framework set up for exploration?

We are trying to set up a framework and evaluation process. We try to balance things so that we have 50 percent or so fee-based work and 50 percent risks, new ventures, startups, or equity-based projects. More than anyone in the studio, I definitely tend to lean toward risky, exciting projects—the kind that most people are not comfortable with.

The LUNATIK business is a good business. It's still a startup, but it takes a little bit of pressure off the fee-based work, allowing us to take more risks with other startups. Whether they're our own or people we partner with.

We are trying to get more science around how we decide what to take on, but it's tough. We get a lot of requests now from startups who want us to do something for them, and we have to vet out the ones that are crazy versus the ones that are legitimate. We have a couple of ventures we are excited about in the MedTech area, where we are not only designing for but also investing in these companies. One is a cardio project, and one is an infectious-disease control project.

The cardio project is for a start-up called AUM Cardiovascular, who's vision is to eliminate needless death due to coronary artery disease. The other project is a startup called Surfacide, in which we are creating a system that fights hospital-acquired infections (HAIs). HAIs are the superbug infectious diseases that kill more people in hospitals every year than the two leading cancers. If you go into the hospital for anything these days, you've got a 5 percent chance of contracting an HAI. We are working on a UV light system that will bombard and kill these superbugs at a cellular level versus using chemicals and drugs, which superbugs become drug resistant to.

What is your process like?

Working with startups, you have to use your instincts and what you've acquired along the way. Of course, with medical, you have to do the research, and that's why we do trials. I've done some small medical projects at IDEO, but you can't always follow the same process. You learn the ideal process along the way and then adapt and morph based on how much money and time you have. You can never follow the same script. Over time, you just have to be able to adapt and evolve.

We definitely have more of an organic process. When it comes to fee-based work, we have a phase 'one-through-four' kind of process. Working with startups is different; you never know what the day-to-day will bring.

Something will come up and you'll have to shift gears, change directions and not let it freak you out. You have to be wired that way. You have to thrive on chaos. Startups are chaos, and you have to be comfortable with that.

What attributes have you noticed that have helped people thrive in this environment?
You have to have courage, and you have to be fearless. You can't be afraid to be comfortable outside of your comfort zone, and you have to have curiosity. It's really important to be curious about all aspects of business.

If you're an entrepreneur, it's very hard to be designing full time and running a business. I found out the hard way after running two manufacturing startups. I knew that if I ever wanted to design again I'd better find some people to help me run the business.

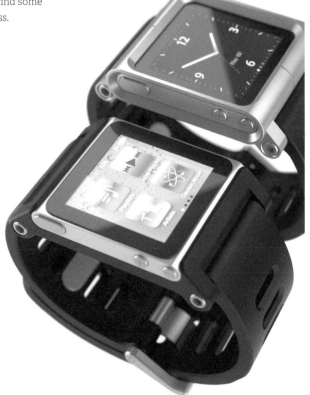

TikTok+LunaTik, Watches

You will get sucked into the financials, the management and the production, and you'll never get back to designing, and then you'll be a one-product company. You have to plan ahead and surround yourself with people who can take it, but you also have to have the curiosity about how business works.

If you aren't interested in the business side of design and entrepreneurship, then you probably shouldn't do it. In Erik Calonius' book, *Ten Steps Ahead: What Separates Successful Business Visionaries From the Rest of Us*, he says, 'Courage is what separates visionaries from dreamers.' Many people have ideas, but they don't all have the courage to go and do it. The ability to take risks is what separates entrepreneurs from dreamers.

You have to be yourself, and you have to be humbly confident. When talking to partners or investors, humble confidence and credibility are necessary to connect with people who are basically going to make your dream a reality.

You've talked about how you're attracted to risk. What would you say is the biggest risk you've taken in your career?
One of the biggest risks was definitely Uncommon. Uncommon is a customization brand that I cofounded, and it was the first to crack the code of one-off mass customization on premium accessories products.

I probably worked the hardest I have ever worked on something. I worked 24/7 for more than a year on Uncommon. We launched with branding, product design, engineering, operations, material development, print collateral, a curated artist community, packaging — everything. We did all of that in five months. That blew people away in the industry who were trying to figure out one-off customization. They said, 'How the hell is he doing this in five months?' That process entailed more than a million dollars worth of studio fees, and then I walked away with

nothing after getting screwed in a bad partnership. That was painful. People ask whether that experience drove me to pursue TikTok+LunaTik. On one hand, absolutely. It was a horrible experience, but at the same time, if I were still completely immersed in Uncommon, I would have never done TikTok+LunaTik. It would have just been a CAD project that I played around with on the side.

I signed away my ownership in Uncommon on the 2nd of November, 2010. My wife made me promise no more startups until the following spring, and I signed a coaster at dinner one night and said, 'But I have this one other idea... well it's this kind of watch thing.' She said, 'Oh, that's silly — whatever, go ahead and do that.' On Nov. 16, I launched the watch kits on Kickstarter.

Who are your mentors, and what is your role as a mentor for startups?
My dad was a huge, initial influence on my design and my life. I also studied with, was exposed to, and spent time with a range of influential designers, just serendipitously throughout my career. I sat down with them and heard what they had to say. I didn't always prescribe to everything they said, but I definitely took what I could and let it inform my process and philosophy. I was fortunate to learn from influential designers such as Philippe Starck, Ross Lovegrove, Julian

Brown and Stefano Giovannoni, but I would say it's my peers and coworkers who have influenced me the most. Ed Boyd, former Global Creative Director at Nike, now the head of design at Dell, has been my biggest mentor and supporter along the way. When I designed the Nike Presto watches, he told me, 'Do what you think is right and apologize later.' When I heard that, a switch went on inside of me that you have to do what is necessary to make what you believe in real. My process as a mentor is constantly evolving. I learn from the people I work with both in and outside of the studio, and they learn from me. I might be doing back-to-back meetings and making all kinds of progress, but if I'm not actually creating something or solving problems, then I get kind of grumpy. I am a leader by example. I like being side-by-side in the trenches, and I love getting my hands dirty at the factory during the manufacturing process. I'm not big on presentations and conferences and don't really like doing them. I know it's a thing that people do at certain points in their careers, but I'd much rather have the work.

AUM Cardiovascular's Cadence™ Device

LunaTik, iPod Nano Watch Conversion Kit

That's what I like about the fact that we can now tell stories through digital platforms—you can get your story out there without having to get in front of a bunch of people. At the end of the day, I'm an introvert. I've had to work very hard to get comfortable presenting and talking to people.

If you want to make your dream a reality, you have to be a salesperson and put yourself out there, or else it just won't happen.

Entrepreneurship makes people do what they have to do even, if it's outside of their comfort zones.

What excites you most about where the process is headed?

It's a very exciting time for everyone in design to use these new tools, whether you digitally print an on-demand book or launch a project on Kickstarter, it is great to see all of the dots connecting—design becomes even more powerful as they connect. Transparency is super important today, whether you're a Kickstarter project, a startup or a corporation, really. I think companies have forgotten how to be transparent. It's so nice to be able to put a face to a company and connect the consumer to the brand. People love to be involved in the design process. Today's tools allow the consumer to be a part of that process. The journey is as important or more important than the destination. Let the consumer be a part of that journey.

Duane King | Designer, Huge / KingCoyle | Portland, OR

Edits by Edit, Screenprinted Poster

"Really I have no separation between the two. Life is work,
and work is life. I do what I love, and I love what I do."

Duane King

Thinking Is Living

Duane King is a designer, thinker and writer. Together with Ian Coyle, Duane ran a creative studio and consultancy based in Portland, Ore., that merged with digital agency Huge to create Huge/KingCoyle, an innovation lab focused on design, culture and craft. His work is a combination of smart concepts and well-crafted execution. He also is a prolific writer and a proponent of the written word.

Duane is the founder of Thinking for a Living, a publisher and curator of thought-provoking design content and creator of meaningful experiences.

Could you tell us a bit about your background and how you came to design?

Despite a childhood filled with drawing what I would later learn are called logos, I had no idea that design was a profession until much later in life. In high school, I fell in love with typography while working at a silkscreening shop, where I would have to reproduce type by hand. It was then that I first noticed that an 'O' wasn't simply a circle — and that its shape varied from typeface to typeface. Soon thereafter, I discovered graphic design. I then moved to a little town called Denton, just north of Dallas, and enrolled in the University of North Texas.

Upon graduation, all of the late nights invested in my portfolio were rewarded when my work was selected as the best of my class. It made getting my first job easy. But easy didn't last long. I was instantly immersed in the fast-paced world of design and advertising, and began to work my first 100-hour weeks. Admittedly, I was surprised when I was eventually asked: 'What do you know about the computer?'

Computers weren't part of my education. Instead, I spent my time focused on technique, process and hand skills. So I quit the job at the design studio, got a loan for my first Macintosh, and started to work at Kinko's. Every night after work, I would spend hours on the computer. Eventually, I ended up getting a call from a friend at a local design studio, who asked, 'Do you know Illustrator?'

I didn't, but I said I did. I downloaded the program that very night and began to poke around. I reported for work the next day and did my best. But inevitably I had to spill the beans and admit that I was still learning the program. I had, however, proven my adaptability and willingness to learn. My journey from not knowing to knowing continues to this day.

You ran a studio in collaboration with Ian Coyle in Portland that focused on design, culture and craft. Can you describe your collaboration and how your practice has benefitted from a partner?

Years ago when in Santa Fe, my firm was looking for a design and development partner for a site for an Italian glassware manufacturer. That was when I first met Ian. The moment we began working together, it was clear that we were onto something special. With a relationship built on respect, honesty and trust, we found our skills and interests complemented each other well. Challenged and reinvigorated, I closed my studio and moved to Oregon to pursue the next phase of my life. Within three days of our arrival, we became official Portlanders when we landed our first project for Nike. Ian and I normally have about 48 hours to concept and two weeks to deliver a prototype for our clients. As a result, our design process has evolved to be decidedly nonlinear. We jump into a hybrid of prototyping and design as soon as an idea begins to form. Much of the time, we explore our preliminary ideas in code in an attempt to find the boundaries for design and interaction. Then, we return to Photoshop in order to create the visual concepts. Once we define the voice, we switch back to code and refine the prototype. The cycle continues until we eventually have a polished final product. Although continually in flux, our process has proven successful and rewarding.

In a 2009 interview, you talked about how large agencies and studios are not sustainable business models for the future, and that all the tools and resources that they used to have exclusive access to are now available to all. You said, 'I feel that small, decentralized groups of like-minded specialists are the logical progression for our still young industry.' Do you think this is happening?

At times, given the never-ending desire to label and categorize talent, it can be easier for a client to understand what a single person does. Conversely, there are still many occasions when a client has more faith in an agency. Creating that same sense of reliability can be a hurdle for a small organization.

There are times when you must scale to meet the needs of your client, but the challenge is to do so without losing yourself in the process. Often, the easiest answer is to partner with other small teams. It's always a balancing act.

You've since merged your studio, King/Coyle, with the advertising agency Huge to create the design innovation lab Huge/KingCoyle. Why did you decide to merge, and what excites you most about the potential for the lab?

Coincidentally, the merger speaks to exactly the point I mentioned in the interview from 2009. Over the years, our clients at King/Coyle have grown to include many Fortune 100 companies. As result, we needed to expand to meet our client needs.

Huge is an industry leader, and our partnership affords us access to some of the top talent in the world — as well as the scalability required for our projects. It's the best of both worlds; we can be small and nimble, as well as large and powerful. And the lab environment maintains the experimental approach to design and development for which we're known.

What resources are available for small groups of specialists to learn about the business side of design? A side of our industry, which large agencies understand.

The resources are out there; we just have to be open to investigating them. We must learn to be open-minded about the art of business. It can be easy to shove the topic to the wayside as it lacks the veneer of design, but ultimately, it's unavoidable. Success dictates an understanding of business, or the success will be fleeting. Ask questions of your mentors and peers, learn about invoicing and proposal writing, read business journals. You must speak the language of a world that is larger than that of the design community alone.

You define yourself as a designer, a thinker and a writer. How does your focus on writing impact your design practice?

Design is communication and writing is, too. While I've always been a fan of the written word, that admiration has primarily been from afar, and mostly in the form of reading. But over the years, as I began to master some of the basics of graphic communications, I began to explore writing and communication further.

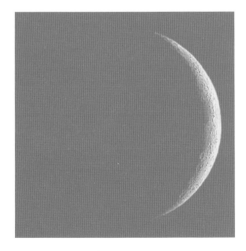

Moon Phase, Thinking for a Living

At first, my interest was born from the need for holistic creative concepts that integrated design, interaction and copywriting. That interest was spurred on by articles that I wrote for Thinking for a Living. And since people keep asking me to write, I keep at it. Writing feels just like design when it has intent and purpose.

Although my tendency is toward visual communication, I am a storyteller by nature. Writing is just another way for me to exercise that skill.

Thinking for a Living is a wonderful resource of design writing, a bookshelf and a curated blog that you made with some of your peers. Can you talk a bit about the motivation for this self-initiated project?
Thinking for a Living was created for those who believe that while design is a profession, it's above all a passion. And as passionate graphic designers, we are obliged to ourselves, our industry and our clients to provide creative solutions that have persuasive branding messages as well as emotional power and aesthetic value. Great design is an art, not a commodity or a formula. It's a structure and process that needs to be tested and re-examined as it evolves.

The site attempts to aggregate varied influences because brilliance exists in the broad search and the clever linkage of one seemingly unrelated event to another. If you see an object that makes you think of another, the two together are an idea. Heraclitus, a Greek philosopher in 500 B.C. pointed out, 'A wonderful harmony arises from joining together the seemingly unconnected.'

What platforms best encourage designers to share their perspectives through writing? Has Thinking for a Living found a successful framework for this?
I think that one of the biggest challenges is the attention span of our audience. As designers,

we skim and scan. We skip from item to item with only a brief passing glance. Collecting, at times, seems more valued than comprehending. Many times, the best writing online is passed over in our haste. Fortunately books have a built-in element of a peaceful pause. It's not called reading for pleasure without due reason; although I'm sure it still grows ever harder for most of us to find a quiet moment to reflect.

Of course, the other hurdle is finding the time to write. It's hard for a successful designer to find the time to do so as they are typically doing what they do best — design. It should come as no surprise. We are, after all, designers by trade. Personally, I am wary of becoming someone who talks about making things rather than someone who makes them.

Many of our contributors have said that when they follow their passions, work and life often become inseparable. Your foreword for *Bracket: Craft* talks about how true craftsmanship takes time. How to you approach your design-life balance?
Really I have no separation between the two. Life is work, and work is life. I do what I love, and I love what I do. For me, the line between design and life is blurry, and potentially nonexistent. Time seems to disappear when I am engrossed in the playful pursuit of a good idea. I truly do lose myself in my work.

Do you consider yourself an entrepreneur?
I do. I used to shrug off notions of being a businessman, but I now realize that entrepreneurship requires great creativity. If you think coming up with ideas from scratch is hard, try coming up with operating capital. Talk about getting creative.

Thinking for a Living, Website

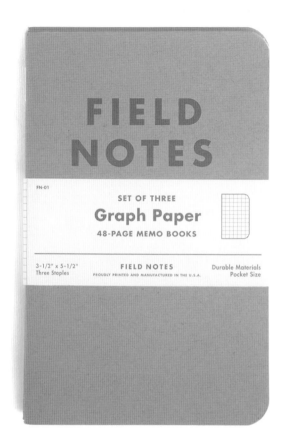

Field Notes, Memo Book

"We have a skill set, and we can go invent things."

Aaron Draplin

Hammer All Night Long

Aaron Draplin just wants to make stuff that his dad will understand. Stuff that's simple, shows a sense of restraint, and looks good on a billboard and a 1-inch button. He's a man with a bold mouth who shares his opinions freely and puts out work that he believes in. He's the founder of Draplin Design Co. (DDC) and Field Notes Brand, a DDC/Coudal Partners collaboration.

Aaron challenges designers to invent their own world and to get out there and get dirty; in everything he does, he lives his motto: "Work hard, and do good work for good people."

We know a lot of your story; can you give us insight into how you got into design?
Here's the thing; Before I had an inkling to what it would take to make it in graphic design, projects had this seductive quality to them, and that got me hooked—be it a backstage pass to a buddy's party or something else. It's only going to cost you 10 bucks to print something out, and then you get it laminated for a couple more bucks. You make this one little object for this little kid's birthday party in some little town, and suddenly the party is that much more fun.

It's always fascinated me—the act of making graphic design. It's something I didn't have to do. That little object was for fun, and then I could use that in a portfolio. Isn't that interesting?

I didn't have to wait in line for some client job to load up my portfolio. I couldn't show a lot of the client work from those beginning years because I was on a leash and getting beat down. That's life. You have to understand, you have one foot in that shit; you slay it, and take it on the chin. You try to be creative about doing a good job and getting what the client needs done. But my favorite designers always had another foot in—not just making rent—but making things. They produced. From early on, I didn't have a carrot on a stick saying, 'You'll get a job; you'll be schooled; you'll be gainfully employed.' It was a hobby first, to learn and to emulate the guys I liked. Oh man, there was some gnarly shit I made back then that I will never show... but, that's what you do when getting started, you know?

In 1995, I saw my first *HOW* and *CommArts* magazines. I was 23 and learning this new craft. I got the sense that at some point I'd be able to apply it to something. At that point I was just OK with doing whatever it took to survive. Every opportunity was just this weird icing on the cake. I didn't take it with a grain of salt. I was enamored with the idea that I got to do this stuff, not that I was entitled to do it. Because that's where it gets scary you know? Grad school teaches you that you are the greatest thing coming out of MICA, pica, STD, DDC, whatever. Then you get out of school, and some yahoo tells you to make coffee. Ha!

I went to art school. The kids get out; they are hypertalented, and there's this sense that they'll be handed something. That's fine, but some of them aren't talented but still expect the big gig. I came into that environment, and on my way up, I had to paint futon covers and letter chalkboards, and I understood a real tradesmen quality — I had to do whatever it took to pay my rent. Pushing that into when I started to practice for myself, it only made sense that you'd make a little extra cash, and you'd make a little T-shirt that says Draplin Design Company. Make things that fuck with the 'bottom-line-ism' of what you're doing. You're not supposed to give away a T-shirt for free. You know, you meet people and share the little extra that you have, which might just be the ability to say, 'Hey, take this stupid pencil that costs 18.5 cents. If you sharpen this pencil, and start a stroke, it goes for 565 yards of mark making until it's a little nub. That's pretty cool.' Give something away to stoke someone out. I like to be able to say, 'Here, this is for you...' I'm always proud to be able to defy the 'bottom-line-ism' everyone else hides behind. 'You like this? Take it. It's for you!'

I watched my dad do that; it was never about trying to make a dollar on it; it was just that quality of, 'I get to do this.'

All of this goes into Field Notes. I made my first bunch by screen printing them on a gocco machine. I'm a fucking black belt with that thing. I did five colors on a card a decade ago. White as the flash layer, then four layers of CMYK. I could make something very real, just simply printing black on this little thing or some boss French Paper, and it looks real. Tactile. And then you realize, it almost looks like toner. Ha! How dumb is that? To print black ink with a gocco printer? So dumb.

I made my first bunch of Field Notes that way, and I could control that thing. I never thought, 'Oh, I could put these things in a little packet and sell them.' They were just to give away to my friends. From that perspective, you're an inventor. You come from this place where it's just fun to make stuff. We're tasked every day as designers, or whatever, to make this thing, for this much money. You make $38,000 a year to make something for company 'X,' and we say OK. When you're on the clock, and someone says, 'Here, make this' from 9 to 5, it sucks. But when you're at home buck naked on a fucking Saturday night, making some cool shit, it's different. Making things is fun.

The purity of that transaction is something we can forget about... or something we pay a bunch of money to go to a conference to be reminded about.

Do you think the ability to invent is something a designer either has or doesn't have? How would you encourage that in designers?
It's one thing for me to sit here and say, 'Do this,' because it might unlock a door for you or be fun. But you've got to have it in you. If you don't, it shows. Who am I to say it's right or wrong? But there's just this fastidious quality to people, and you can smell it on them. People who give you a little hand-cut business card.

The design might not even be your cup of tea, but they've taken the extra step to do it. Or, the guy who made this really nice letterpress card for two bucks each. There's a wow element there. They believed enough to spend two bucks on each card. But there's something nice and dirty about the kid who didn't have any money but was able to make something out of it. That kid's going to go a long way because he or she knows how to take nothing and make something. I'm not going to point fingers, of course. But OK, I'm going to point a couple motherfuckin' fingers. You can see a sense of entitlement sometimes. People who ask, 'Why would I do that? Go that extra mile?' They don't see the beauty of that hard work. Or that ingenuity. My favorite designers do what they do during the day to make a fucking living and then start at 6 p.m. at night making what they love, often for no loot or reward. That's what I saw before I saw people hating their jobs, or hating how much hard work this actually takes.

That sounds familiar to us.
Great. Get fucking used to it. What else would you be doing? You could be sitting in a bar drinking or fucking around. There's balance in life, sure. But, you could also be this creative entity. It's a sickness for me. It's turned into this thing where I can get way ahead and use it all in more fun and wild ways to make more shit. I have a platform to evangelize or something. But what you guys don't see is that as soon as we're done here, I'll go hammer away on my projects. It's not anything romantic; it's for components for a catalog that will further us along toward completion. It's not fun, but I get some music going, and I just hammer.

See what I'm getting at? Being gracious, or being cognizant that when you get to do it for fun it's pretty cool. And then, when shit sucks, you gotta make it cool, too. I'm not happy building catalog pages, but I get paid way more than I should and love the guys I work for.

Cobra Dogs, Logo

It's probably under market price, but it's probably way better than what I could do with my own devices. I don't know how to explain it, but I have a hard time deciding what sucks from what is fun. I'm in the middle of a project right now that should be the greatest thing in the world, but it's killing me 'cause I showed some cool stuff, and they said they didn't know whether they liked it. But you gotta keep pounding; I won't give up. I don't know how to give up. As much as I don't wanna go touch the thing today, I'll work on it tonight, from 9 until 3 in the morning to make the client something killer. That's just part of a good work ethic, you know? In between that time, I'll find time to send off posters or a reprint. I'll figure out orders or figure out other extraneous stuff. Job No. 1 always has to be job No. 1, but I always have jobs two through seven.

I go to speak at these conferences and find myself asking people why they aren't working. I have to juggle that. I find it almost a little wobbly and peculiar to think that a kid has five days to go chill at a conference because they've punched out of their job. I think, 'Oh man, I've created a monster where I can't get away from this stuff, ever.' Pretty sure I have.

It's refreshing that you treat design like any other trade. Is the business side of things a craft as well?

All of this stuff is a craft. I gotta think that this whole thing's days are numbered. I take it all very seriously. I take the idea of locking down an estimate and figuring out timing as a necessary accoutrement to letting someone know they are in good hands. I might be this pantsless behemoth animal behind the scenes, but I'm going to dot every 'i.' I'm going to say thank you in every email, even if they don't notice. When I see people communicate back and forth with people in lowercase, like, without the respect to actually craft a sentence or proper reply? I take the time to make it all something I can be proud of in 10 years. It's a sickness. I understand you just need to say yes or no. But all of that communication is part of the form, of being able to smooth people over, and make them comfortable. I hope it's refreshing when clients see the work, sold through a nice presentation. It doesn't take that much longer, but it's important. It actually makes it a bit more streamlined for myself. I know how to pound them into little

Gary, Illustration

makes it a bit more streamlined for myself. I know how to pound them into little presentations and systems that I've built.

To answer your question, absolutely of course. It's dicey when it doesn't look like you took the time. Say you work on a client for two different projects and things look different each time. I mean, listen. I dodge, lie, cheat and steal like any other motherfucker to get through projects, but I want them to feel that they are cared for. That's it. I hope that they do. And they are. I show them the work that went into their project. Sure, maybe they don't know that I'm crying in a hotel room in Belfast, but I want them to feel cared for.

Can you talk a little bit about how you and Jim Coudal collaborated together to get Field Notes started? Did Jim spur you on or change your mind? Do you have thoughts for designers who want to make their own products instead of work for clients?
Before I knew Jim, I thought his tone was cool, almost a little scary. Not pompous but forthright. He would say things like, 'We are going to do the work that best suits what we do.' Now that's different. 'Then we'll morph into whatever you want for us to make money.' I smelled that on his studio instantly.

I was just a fan of this idea that when you went to Jim's site or shop, you didn't even know what Coudal Partners did. That's a strategy also. They provide you with links, cool stuff, resources, and they have this spirit of sharing. You think these guys are just aggregating stuff all day long or something? But no. They're fucking backhanding you with awesome ideas and products, and then all of a sudden you're like, 'I want my name set in fucking pins...[Pinsetter].' Now, why do I need my name set in pins? I don't know. It's just this neat little gift. I bought a bunch of Jewel Boxes [Jewelboxing] as gifts for mix tapes I was making. I made them for friends. You're

supposed to use them for a pitch, but I used them for presents. I like that Coudal made me aware of that thing. And then, I just contacted him. I said I wanted to meet him, and he kind of said the same thing—'Thank you, and we were watching you, too, Draplin.' That's it. I went in there and showed him a couple things I was working on. It was never to impress him. I was just like, 'Take some of these; they're cool,' and gave him a stack of the early Field Notes. He saw how to make them into something real, and I didn't. I'm still excited just to have a stack, at that point. What he's taught me is that we have a skill set, and we can go invent things. It's good to remind yourself that. If you can figure out a better way to make a potato chip than a potato chip we have now, go fucking do it. You've got to put capital up, and research and things, and that's what Jim does. He puts his money where his mouth is. He has my respect as a pioneer and the spirit of go-getting-it-ness. They just know how to go get it, and then they make it theirs. The tone is positive, and a little prickly, and they aren't going to do it a certain way because it's the easiest way to do it. They do it the right way. That's a seductive thing to me. They have the guts to do that. You're not supposed to do that, but they just fucking put their foot down and do it. Jim's a smart guy who understands how to build things, burn things down, build things up and fund things. He understands the big picture. He can do that. There's a bit of an elite quality to that. Only so many guys know how to brand build like that. I feel pretty lucky to collaborate with that kind of greatness.

I love the Charles Spencer Anderson Design Co. They made a whole line that was just 'Chuck's line of cool shit.' They made a mouse pad for designers. It 'backhand-ily' showed me their stuff, but it was just a cool piece of meat clip art or something. You know, everyone needs a mouse pad, and you get to pick a CSA-designed one. How great is that? It's amazing. They were just a group of smart people making cool things. It didn't matter whether you knew they made logos or managed big design projects. They were just great. Like House Industries. It doesn't even matter that they're making logos or fonts or whatever; they're just cool. They're making cool shit. They were like this clubhouse or something, and I just wanted to be a part of what they were doing. I wanted to ask them for a job, but I didn't want to live in fucking Delaware. I went to House on a fall tour and told them I was there to buy some fonts. I was man enough to show up. They let me in, and we hung out for a couple hours. It was really cool. I left there thinking, 'These guys are really lucky to do what they do.' But no, they just went and grabbed it. It's a scarier proposition than a lot of their colleagues who work for clients, but they actually invent shit. They also work for clients, but you don't see it. You see all the font sets and shit. Great guys, so smart, goddammit.

How do you take something that has an audience and try to monetize it? When do you make that choice?

Will you buy a record that you love? I'll pay 10 bucks for it. How much is that fucking stupid-ass sandwich you're eating? Get realistic about things you spend your money on. Field Notes costs $9.95! I'll remind people, 'What'd you pay for that stupid coffee? Six bucks?' That's stupid. Our priorities are so messed up.

If I could monetize my nerdy love of looking at logos in Ireland, I probably would. But on second thought, why would I? It's a little thing. I just wanna put it up and share it, and say, 'Look at what I saw! Take this, get inspired, and go make a great logo.'

You might like ornate shit, but I like thick-lined things. But let me see your ornate shit. I hope people enjoy the fact that I just freely share stuff. But, then I say, 'Hey, you like that? Go buy a fucking T-shirt.' It needs to come with a little back door. By the way, here's something else. What's that little 'fucking-with-the-bottom-line-ism' element that people are going to like?

A button thing, or notepad or whatever. It defies the 10 bucks that they spent. Give them something extra, whenever you can.

I go back to buying records. They came with buttons, stickers and a patch. Little things they didn't have to include, but they did. It's pennies on the dollar in the big picture, but that wins the hearts of people. Every little Field Notes thing that we make comes with something extra. Every single time. Because I still get pumped by that. I have mountains of buttons. If I get one more fucking 1-inch button, I'll kill somebody. But it's still really great to get that little surprise, right? It's great. That defies the situation where everyone else is going to charge you for every fucking thing. You want ice in your glass? We have a web form for that.

But you just don't see that out there these days. Every little thing is accounted for and sweated out. Every time I make fun of the rigidity of all this hipster shit, some Field Notes vendor flips me off. Ha! But it's just the idea of sameness I don't like. Before, everyone was some coy name. Like naming their company 'Something Nothing' or some coy shit. Well, isn't that fucking ironic? Or some funny word play? I reacted against that because it felt put-on. A year before that, I was fucking 'Draplindustries.' How clever is that? That was stupid. My email was so long. Then, design just became a lot of put-on, like, 'We're smarter than we are.' They aren't smart. They're just good at putting icing on the cake. There's no icing on my cake; it's just a good cake — I hope, at least. We don't give you icing! Lot of metaphors here, but I waded through a lot of icing for a while and didn't get good cake. That's fine, and I understand how things go with trends and things. It's trending right now, like, to name your deal 'Something Supply Company.' There's this sameness you

DDC, Merchandise List Detail

fought for it when it wasn't cool. I'm not backing off that. This is my story. It's not fashion or the latest trendy way to name a company. I take the whole bad joke of being the Draplin Design Co. very seriously and still fuck with it constantly. When we're done here with this interview, I go back to it, and I live it. It's a monster I created for myself. I'm not necessarily happy about that, but the only way to get out of the hole is to stop digging. There's some fucking sentiment for you. Stop digging, and start climbing out, you know. Here I am in Belfast, out in the world. I could go to a museum today or some other shit, but the need to work doesn't change. The clients never let up. 'Where's the shit, Draplin? You took money from us and said we'd have it.' Ok, done, I'll do it. Like this morning, I walked over to this little convenience store to gear up. I got a couple chocolate bars and a couple waters because I don't wanna drink out of the toilet. I just wanna be comfortable in that hotel room. You gotta go ramp up. Get snacks and things. Tonight I'll hear, 'Why didn't you go to the museum today, Draplin?' Because I got my work done today! I'll be happy if I can say that.

Is it hard for you, when you meet other designers to decide when it's a Jim Coudal or it's just someone who wants something? You know, like us?

Not at all! I'm here to make friends. Wanting things? Like interviews and shit? They are all opportunities. I've been burned a couple times. People are excited to meet me, which is still a weird thing. But I'll forever be like that when I meet someone from a band, and they don't know what I do. I gotta watch myself and hold my tongue and stuff. I try and remember that now that I'm in this position where people come up to me a lot. I try to be slow. If it's a young kid all freaked out, I try not to be to foreboding because I'm like this huge, fucking man mountain. Like when I meet some young designer. Do I

have more design in my little fucking pinky than they do in their whole body? Probably; but maybe not. Maybe they have more. Hold your horse, kid! Give me a couple years to save my money, then you can come and kick my ass. But as far as being able to pick the things I do like this? Media is all an opportunity; any press is good press. I look at this as an odd privilege. You know who does that, too? Kate Bingaman-Burt; she's the shit. She exudes this quality that design can be fun. She can always find time for any little student or for that top-gun student. She really knows how to guide them both. I just think that's a beautiful calling, or vocation or something. I've been told, 'Draplin, you'd be a good teacher.' That really touched me. I'd think that people would be scared of me or something. Like, I'm an intimidating presence or something.

I've been striking the iron while it's been hot for a long time. I'm ramping down a bit. I'm going to quit in a year. It's not like I'm going to start a new life. It's more like I'm going to slow down fucking around for top dollar. How much do I need to live? My life costs about eight grand a year. For insurance, living expenses, going to 'Whole Paycheck.' That's what I call Whole Foods. Man, my arm hurts from grabbing for my wallet. Fucking assholes. But you know, what does your life mean? How much do you need to live? You gotta be insured, gotta have a car, gotta pay rent, gotta have home insurance. Make a list of all the stuff you have to have and add it up. And say, 'OK, I gotta come up with $3,300 a month.'

Why am I working so much to afford some idea that this all costs ninety grand a year? It doesn't. I don't need it. Shouldn't you spend your life exercising more? Two words that strike fear into a man my size, 'Personal Trainer!' But it's coming; I need some help. Take some shit by the balls, and don't live this life sedentarily like we do. I'm going to do that. It's not about going after these crazy, big projects. I've learned that. What happens when it's not about making the next set's money? Maybe, it's about helping people? I'm really going to contact those Christians in Portland who wash feet. I hope you guys aren't some raving Christian people? But whatever if you are; that's a really brilliant thing that they are doing. That helps people. What do we want to do with our lives? I'm a graphic designer; that's what I make. But I don't know if I want to keep doing it for commercial sources. Will I live the life of a pauper? I might. But, I got a shitload of money in the bank. This jacket was 14 bucks at the Cabela's bargain cave, and it smells like an old fucking sock. I don't need 10 of them, I need one. When I travel, I have a pair of jeans, a sweatshirt, a couple 'under-roos,' six pairs of socks, and I try to keep my shit clean. But I don't need to bring six pairs of jeans; I don't even need to bring two. I have a pair of jeans. Black. They're 4 years old. Why are we spending our money on all this other shit? I step back from all of that and imagine working one day a week to cover my insurance things and shit. Maybe Monday covers my 10 grand a year, and maybe Tuesday covers another 10 or 15, so I can take trips with it. Then on Wednesday, Thursday and Friday, I work for people who need help. Or I fucking take the day off, or I work out or donate some time somewhere.

Like, Mikey Burton. I like the fact that he laughs. He's just a really nice guy. I really root for him. I don't know if he makes a lot of money. I hope he makes a shit-ton, I hope he makes enough where he doesn't have to worry about anything. And Dan Cassaro, too. Those guys are adding some great things to graphic design. We're really lucky to do this. Think about a bunch of people who sell insurance; it's not the same. Mikey makes great posters. I've learned to make a better logo from Mikey Burton, and hell, I can hold my own. There are pieces of Dan Cassaro's shit that I've learned from, too. Little type pieces and shit that knucklehead makes. So good. This is turning into a big ol' slobber fest. Can we be done? Cool. I gotta go hammer on my projects.

Space Shuttle Redesign, Logo

Mikey Burton | Designer, Illustrator | Philadelphia, PA

Freelance Ain't Free, Letterpressed Poster

"I feel really lucky to do what I do. I make things
for a living, and that's really fun. Why should I
be overcritical of that?"

Mikey Burton

Make It Fun

Mikey Burton considers himself lucky to do what he does. He earned his Bachelor of Science and Master of Arts in Visual Communication Design from Kent State University, cofounded the design studio, Little Jacket, and is now a full-time freelancer.

Mikey's "Midwesterny" style features thoughtful visuals executed with limited palettes and textures informed by his interest in analog printing techniques. He designs and illustrates for such clients as The Atlantic, Bloomberg Businessweek *and* The New York Times, *but it's his self-initiated projects that challenge him and lead to unexpected places. His project, the "Freelance Ain't Free" print, has developed into a brand, microsite and movement.*

You got your graduate degree at Kent State and then worked at 160over90. What made you decide to go out on your own, and what were the risks?

I went straight from undergrad to graduate school. One of the reasons that we started our studio, Little Jacket, while we were still in school was just that we wanted to do fun stuff outside of the class work we were already doing. After working with Little Jacket for about five years, I went to 160over90. I'd never worked in a structured environment, and I wanted to see how a business worked for bigger clients.

It was an experience. It was hard, and I worked long hours—the same story anyone will tell you who has worked in advertising—but it allowed me to expand my interests. I started moonlighting as an illustrator in my free time, which was something I had never even thought about and something I wasn't even interested in. I was more interested in being a designer. But I discovered that I loved the pace and quick turnaround time of editorial work. I didn't like the idea of being stuck on one project for five months, and with editorial pieces, I could just produce something, and it was done. I started to think, 'Oh, this is cool. I like doing design, but I also like doing illustration.' I started to talk to an illustration rep about six months before I left just to have a game plan of what I wanted to do next. I thought that I could go out on my own, and by the time I was done at 160over90, I was mentally ready to be on my own. Even though I wasn't financially set, I had been working really hard and doing a lot of outside work, so I thought just maybe I could do it. As soon as I made the jump, I was financially comfortable. I didn't think that would happen right away; I was really nervous about it. I do editorial illustration now, and I always wonder, 'How long is that style or whatever I'm doing gonna be relevant?' That's my biggest fear at the moment.

Have you always had the ambition to do your own thing and be in ownership?

I had always wanted to do something on my own. Even when we started Little Jacket, it was an outlet for us to try our hands at running a business. Little Jacket still exists, and the business is doing really well now, but at the time when I left, I was kind of stubborn in a way; I wanted to see it through and hoped it would become this thing that would eventually make money, but it just never did. I always had the drive, even though I couldn't make it happen right away.

Did you gain insight into how to run a business at 160over90?

I went to 160 to learn more about the business side, and I did; I learned how to sell work. They do really good design work, but the thing that's more impressive is the way they sell ideas.

You learned how to market products?

Yeah. There is such an art in selling and presenting work. That knowledge has been pretty helpful when I speak, and I'm able to talk about my work, at least somewhat.

Do illustrators need agents to be successful?

Not necessarily. You can just use the Internet and social media to promote yourself. You have all of these tools at your disposal to get yourself and your work out there. I respect that.

That said, I like the representation. My agent, Scott Hull, constantly holds clients' hands, puts out fires, takes care of contracts, manages expectations, sets up meetings, gets the most competitive rates out of jobs, and does a hundred other things I don't have time for. It's also nice to have a sounding board there to talk through the details of a job and to have somebody there to back you up.

I did a project last year and never received payment, and he spent the whole year following up with them until we got the money. Halfway through, I would have personally just given up and called it a loss, so it's great to have someone to be steadfast. Or, when people plagiarize my work, he can turn a profit out of a bad situation.

What was the motivation behind your self-initiated Freelance Ain't Free project? Are you working on other self-initiated projects outside of client work?

I really love letterpress, and I really like the idea of creating a product. This all came together for me with Freelance Ain't Free. Side projects really help keep the lights on and help you get a little extra money.

New Covers for Old Books was your thesis project at Kent State?

I redesigned the covers for classics such as *The Great Gatsby, Animal Farm* and *Lord of the Flies*. And there's a whole story behind that because I got a really bad grade on that project due to a terrible paper that accompanied the design work. A few years later, Steven Heller featured the project on his blog, The Daily Heller, and he featured my sketchbook in his book *Graphic: Inside the Sketchbooks of the World's Great Graphic Designers*.

People noticed it then. Out of Print Clothing approached me, and they turned some of the designs into T-shirts. Freelance Ain't Free was something I did for fun. I really like letterpress printing, as a lot of designers do. When I was home in Ohio, I wanted to print something, so I wrote down a couple of ideas in my sketchbook and decided, 'Oh, I'll just make one when I'm home.' I was at the Cranky Pressman office with my friend Keith Berger, and I said, 'Can I just print something?' He gave me some paper, and I said, 'I'll do Freelance Ain't Free.' Doing free work is fine; I'm fine with that when I love the cause, and I'll help out self-initiated, self-motivated projects. But big corporate clients will contact you and ask, 'Can you do this? And this? Oh, and I only have, like, 200 bucks.' And you're like, 'Really?'

Instead of putting the Freelance Ain't Free posters in a web store, I made a little site up out of it because it's an idea people can get behind.

Freelance Ain't Free, Badge

I put the posters up, and then I put a comp of a T-shirt, and the project got passed around a bit.

That's the 160over90 type of selling right? You didn't have those T-shirts made when you put the comp up there?

Yeah, and then I produced them after. It's not like anything too crazy has come out of it, but I sold a decent amount of T-shirts.

I had a client that was really late on payment. I sent them a shirt to be funny. Literally the next day, they sent me a check for the payment. Seriously though, it's really important to do personal projects. I make time when I can. Whenever I sit down to do one, they always end up going somewhere else than expected.

Do you work on side projects whenever you can, or is there a strategy to make time for self-initiated projects?

Whenever I can. I forced myself to do the last one, and it made me want to do more. I get so busy, but I can't say no. No matter what it is. Usually, I'll just say, 'Yes, yes. I'll take that.' I have a really hard time saying no to anything that's worth it — especially with editorial stuff. You do it, you're done, and it's money. I think it's my hard-working, Midwestern roots — my parents are self-employed, and they never turn down work. Whenever I tell my dad I had to pass on a job because I'm 'too busy,' he just tells me to work harder. I'm going to try to say no more and come up with a few more of my own ideas to make money instead of taking on all of the client work I can.

You talked about the fear of your illustration style getting old. What are your thoughts on seeing similarities and trends in the work on sites such as FFFFOUND! or dribbble?

I try to do different styles for different people. Sometimes, I'll have ideas that I try to do a little differently for people; sometimes they dig it, and sometimes they don't. I think the difference between a trend — whether it's texture or simple geometric shapes — is the idea behind it all. On some level, there's always a nugget of an idea — a visual idea or a visual pun or something. Some people can't do that as well. I hope that's why people come to me — because my work is a little more thoughtful than just a trendy style. My work, at least since college, has always been kind of textural because I was always into poster art. Geekposters.com was the dribbble of years ago. People would talk about the design, post work and give feedback. I never thought of texture as a trend, I just thought, 'I really like letterpress printing; I really like the quality of the print that comes out of it. How can I make that into my work?' I arrived at the simple two-colored illustration style I do now when I started doing work in grad school; I started designing with printing mind. I had to make the most out of the two or three colors. There is so much stuff in the world; there are so many sites that share work, and we are so impatient as people that we not only have to see people's portfolio work, but we have to see what they're working on, so we have dribbble. I'm sure at some point that will change, and something new will come along. It's hard to see those trends and not wonder, 'When will what I'm doing be up?' But I try to constantly develop and adapt with time. I started out as a designer; then I did advertising; now I'm doing illustration. I don't know what the next thing will be.

What do you think about the way we see all of this work out of context? We don't hear the backstory or know the problem the designer was trying to solve.

You can look at a lot of work, and say, 'This is cool,' but it's not often that you gain meaning and insight from portfolio shots. I always want to talk more about process. I feel like I have a lot of good ideas when I do illustration work, and people like to see that process, too.

I think my final work looks nice, and it's always really refined and polished. But there are always 20 other ideas that people didn't pick. I want to talk more about that. I think process is also a selling point to art directors because people like to see the weird ideas you come up with.

It also instills value in the end if they can see your design-thinking process.
Totally. Much of design and illustration is more about the process than the end result.

What about writing to share your process and your thoughts?
I don't know. I think design writing is kind of weird. Writing about design can be really self-absorbed. Some people can do it really well, and it's not that I don't value what I do, I just don't want to talk about it as much. I kind of just want to make things. If I wrote, it would be about making, things that inspire me, and why they inspire me, more than design in general.

Do you read about design?
I read interviews. If it's relevant, I'll read it. There's good design writing out there, but sometimes it just doesn't do anything for me. I would love to write more about 'making.' I just don't think I'm a strong writer. It takes me a long time to write something. I have trouble tweeting things.

One tweet can take 20 minutes to compose.
Exactly, so, how am I supposed to write whole paragraphs? It's going to take a long time.

The designers who we are inspired by work hard and take everything seriously, but at the same time, they are just having fun. How do we write something that's serious, authentic and impacts people but also reinforces the fact that we're all lucky that we're designers, and it's a pretty fun career?

The Great Gatsby, New Covers for Old Books

I don't know how you do that. That attitude is a great way to look at it. I feel really lucky to do what I do. I make things for a living, and that's really fun. Why should I be overcritical of that?

That's definitely a theme we hear from everyone. When we started this project, we began with a more theoretical, design-criticism angle. Then we met everyone over beers, and said, 'Man, this is awesome. I don't want to go home and write an essay about this. I want to go home and talk about how great this was.'
It's more about housing the content and then letting it speak for itself, not writing about it. Presenting it in a simple form, like what you guys do as designers anyway.

How important is it for an illustrator or designer to have an online network?
It's necessary, and it's a love-hate thing. I hate that of all these networking tools exist, but I wouldn't be where I am without them. They are the best way to communicate with people, especially with illustration work.

That's one reason I think it's good to have both an online network and a representative. I know how to do all these new things, but he still has all these contacts to the way things used to be. I'm sure he has a contact at any place he's ever worked with in the 30-plus years he's been in this business. But it's essential. If you know how to use the web, you can get 30,000-plus followers. You just gotta know how to use the web.

Has the necessity of an online persona created inauthenticity in the way people present themselves?
Online personas are never like the person you actually meet. It's really interesting that you can just create a Twitter profile, put some work up online, get a job from it, and people know who you are. It's weird.

It's like the chicken or the egg with your Internet persona. Does your personality follow your Twitter account, or does your Twitter account follow your personality?
Yes, it's really a strange thing. I'm going to be the old man for a minute and say that so much has changed since I graduated school in 2005. I'm not saying that it's easier. The generation before us says, 'It's easier for you guys.' But I am saying that it's crazy. If you want to be an illustrator, all you need to do is sit down for a day, upload six to 12 pieces to a Cargo Collective site, and with the right kind of networking, you can get illustration work. That can be your job from that simple process, which is crazy. The web's been around for a while now, but when I was out of school, we didn't have that. It's wild.

What are some of your interests outside of design that influence your practice?
Uh, none... I mean, I like food and cooking, trying to see new places, and hanging out with my girlfriend, Carli Dottore. I am also inspired by music. When I was in Ohio, I would always go to thrift stores and record stores, and absorb it all. It seems like kind of shallow stuff. But I don't know; things from the past inspire me.

Real life: The analog version of dribbble.
Yeah, life outside of the Internet. I want to spend more time hunting for inspiration that isn't online, stored easily. When I lecture somewhere, somebody always asks, 'Where do you find inspiration?' And I say, 'The Internet?' And I sound so shitty saying that. I wish I could say, 'I have this special library I go to; it's on a mountain, and I have to go every couple of weeks up the mountain.' I don't know. It's not true. You work, and you drink, and you eat, and you live in the city, and that's about it. Go hang out with friends, recharge your batteries, and then work some more. Have fun.

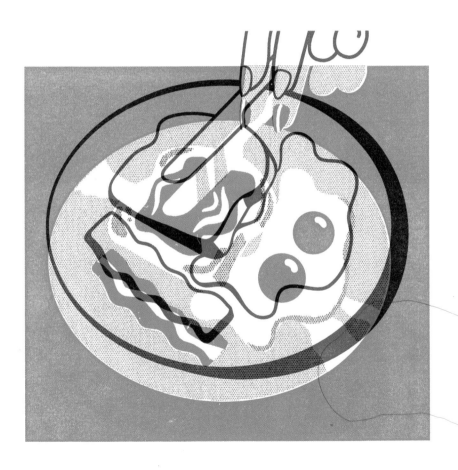

Ariel Pink's Haunted Graffiti, Screenprinted Poster

Mimi O Chun | Design Director, General Assembly | New York, NY

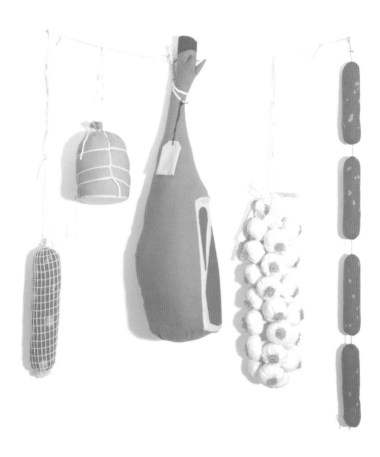

Hipster Emblems, Salumeria

"What defines the entrepreneur is his or her ability to
recognize a problem, need or opportunity in the world
and to have the conviction to want to solve it."

Mimi O Chun

Transcend Your Discipline

Mimi O Chun leads a life driven by dual interests. Her personal work attempts to reveal patterns in banal information too often overlooked. In Hipster Emblems, stuffed artisanal goods, she experiments with media (hand-sewn objects) and meta-narratives (handmaking one-of-a-kind versions of goods) to celebrate a revival of domesticity, of the slow movement and the handcrafted.

This might seem at odds with her day-to-day tasks as the design director of General Assembly, a fast-paced, technology-focused education startup, but it's in this duality that she fully embraces the designer-entrepreneur spirit.

How did you find design?

My father's a computer scientist, and my mother's a painter, so my destiny as a designer was probably a genetically predetermined outcome. Nevertheless, in high school, I felt myself torn between what I assumed were two very distinct directions at the time: design and science. My love for the visual arts was evident at an early age, so pursuing it was a bit of a no-brainer. But I was also interested in forms of neuropsychology — how such intangible notions as mood, personality or cognition could be rooted in the chemical or physical makeup of our brains. I elected to go to Carnegie Mellon because I had been accepted to two schools within the university — College of Fine Arts and Mellon College of Science — and figured it'd be easy for me to switch majors without having to transfer. I started out in the design program, and when it dawned on me that design was, in many ways, the art for the man without an art — that it was something that, not only allowed for, but actually encouraged me to explore other interests — I knew I had found my calling. After graduating, I worked at a number of design studios and consultancies with clients across a range of industries, including education, entertainment, publishing, fashion, technology and hospitality. I maintained a design practice with a friend for about five years until I left New York to pursue my graduate degree.

Hipster Emblems, Small-Batch Pickles

What led you to General Assembly?

I ended up at General Assembly after a chance meeting with Adam Pritzker, one of our founders, while I was at IDEO. We quickly became friends, and when he told me about what he and the other founders were working on—at that point, a nascent idea—I volunteered to help shape the GA brand and experience. I knew very little about the burgeoning tech scene in New York, and my curiosity was piqued. I had always assumed that to be an entrepreneur as a designer meant to start your own client-services business, but as I learned more about tech startups, I began to realize that there was another very real, viable path forward for designers, one that had evaded me for years, and in October 2010, I joined the team full time.

Do you consider yourself an entrepreneur and a designer?

Designer? Yes. Entrepreneur? It's funny. I'll admit I struggle with the idea of calling myself an entrepreneur. Unlike design, which I view as a vocation, entrepreneurship is a little more elusive in its definition.

Since joining the GA team, I've had the opportunity to meet a number of serial entrepreneurs within our community, people who build businesses in wildly disparate industries for the sheer joy of starting something, growing it, exiting and repeating the cycle, and this isn't necessarily a mind-set I can relate to. However, as a designer who enjoys the process of creating an experience and who has always seen authorship and autonomy as the Holy Grail, I would say there's a bit of entrepreneurial spirit that courses through my veins.

General Assembly represents an intersection of technology, business and design. Are successful technology products equal parts technology, design and entrepreneurship?

I'm not sure that I would say that it's an equal split. Certainly you see successful founding teams with various compositions in terms of skill sets. But I do believe that proficiency in these three disciplines—design, technology and entrepreneurship—is critical to the success of companies building digital products.

Do you think entrepreneurship can be taught to designers? How can design education better prepare students to push personal projects into the market? It seems like this conversation is missing from most design curricula...

I think that entrepreneurial instinct is something that transcends discipline. There are equally enterprising writers, designers, technologists, chefs, musicians, etc. as there are those who come from a business background—what defines the entrepreneur is his or her ability to recognize a problem, need or opportunity in the world and to have the conviction to want to solve it. It also requires an inordinate number of soft skills, which are perhaps less easily taught. The most inspiring founders are those who are incredibly self-aware, are quick on their feet, possess a great deal of charisma, and have the fortitude to lead in times of uncertainty—how else could they possibly recruit others to join them on a mission that is statistically unfavorable, or convince investors that their as-of-yet-unrealized vision will one day become a reality? When it comes to the practical skills required to turn an idea into a business—anything from a baseline understanding of finance, fundraising strategies or legal matters, yes, I believe that's something that can be taught. Similarly, I believe that more in-depth domain knowledge relevant to building a product, such as front-end web development or user experience—can also be learned. It requires a different level of commitment, but I think most would say that the reward far outweighs the effort.

One of the things that we're trying to do here at General Assembly, aside from partnering with top practitioners—people who have been out on the front lines and whose points of view have been shaped by their own experiences—is to provide a construct for a community of like-minded people with shared interests to learn among and from one another. Learning doesn't begin or end in the classroom, and knowledge isn't something that's simply passed down from instructor to student—it's a lot more osmotic. How to enable these types of meaningful connections within an online experience is, without a doubt, a tough nut to crack, but it's also one that inspires our team daily. I hope, with this groundswell of new startups, we'll see more designers elect for entrepreneurial routes. It's entirely possible that I'm too close to it here at General Assembly, but I think it's a career path that's virtually impossible to ignore.

It should certainly be part of the discourse within design programs, but I don't believe it should usurp the fundamental skill building or the exploration of craft that occurs at the undergraduate level—for instance, with graphic designers, there's great value in learning the finer points of typography or how to create narratives through things like hierarchy and scale, or composition and pacing. The more mastery one acquires over his or her own craft, the more adept he or she will be in understanding how to create products and experiences that are mindful of, and resonate with, end users.

Why do you think so many designers are turning toward the startup community and away from client services?

Most of us become designers because we have this desire to create experiences, be they products, services, communications, environments, that have palpable impact on the end user. This can be achieved by a number of ways, be they entrepreneurial endeavors, working in-house or through client services. I honestly believe that if I hadn't spent the majority of my career as a consultant, I'd have a much less robust understanding of, for lack of a better word, industry. Every client engagement was an opportunity to not only glimpse the inside of another company, but to engage deeply with new types of content and new industries. I was fortunate in my time at IDEO in that I had the opportunity to work with market leaders; it was only through this exposure that

Hipster Emblems, Succulentia

I could appreciate the full range of opportunities and challenges facing organizations of a certain scale. For those hoping to disrupt an industry with a rich and storied legacy — such as media, art or finance — a deep understanding of how things work within the current landscape is key. You have to understand the lay of the land in order to draw a map. Truthfully, if I can have a moment with my soapbox, I think the allure of startups is one tied closely to the economics and politics of our time. I could be overreaching, but I don't think it's entirely out of the question to see the momentum behind Occupy Wall Street, the outrage over Wikileaks, or the rise of startups as completely unrelated. We've arrived at this juncture in time when we're simply less willing to be complacent or put our blind faith in the status quo — and technology has been a hugely democratizing force in that regard. It's lowered the barriers to entry by providing people not only with effective ways to mobilize and communicate, but actually build things that present a better path forward.

Is the startup culture changing its view toward design?

Definitely. New York is a little different from the Bay in that there are a number of nontechnical founders who are building consumer web and mobile apps in which brand and user experience both play a critical role in differentiating one product from another. It's a crowded space and a zero-sum game.

I am frequently approached by startups looking for referrals to designers. Finding a brand-savvy, visual UX designer — that is, someone who can translate user-based insights into intuitive systems architecture and flows, behaviors and states, and pixel-perfect mockups — is a bit like searching for a unicorn these days. Even more rare if they have front-end fluency.

Do you have advice for designers who want to move away from client services?

Because startups are, by nature, extremely limited in terms of resources, it would be helpful for designers to broaden their reach. The more hats they wear, the more valuable they'll be to any organization. A designer should see him or herself as an advocate for the user — one who creates brands and product experiences that resonate with the user in both pragmatic and emotional terms. This means developing a baseline understanding of user experience, getting familiar with research methods and spending time in the field, learning how to architect information and think through flows, developing wire frames, and gaining familiarity with best practices in usability.

For those designers looking to join existing startups, they should attend local tech events, meetups and hackathons, join communities or coworking spaces where startups tend to congregate, enroll in classes in user research, interaction design or front-end web development, and ask friends to keep their ears open for opportunities. Most great job opportunities will come through word of mouth, and the startup community, at least here in New York, is one of the warmest, receptive and generous I've ever experienced.

For those looking to start a product company, I would recommend that they find a technical cofounder, someone whose skill set is complementary to theirs. Having a thinking partner does wonders for keeping one motivated and on track. They should take every opportunity to talk to anyone who will listen about their idea, maybe start a Kickstarter campaign, but most importantly, they should just start making.

'Make more personal work' and 'stop searching for the perfect time' are two of your personal mantras. Do you have advice

on how to balance a schedule that accommodates both work and play?

For better or worse, most designers are intrinsically motivated while, at the same time, extremely deadline-oriented. For that reason, many of us keep a running tally of rainy-day projects that we'd work on if only we had the time. Accountability is huge—whether that's self-assigning due dates or asking friends to keep you on track. One cheat that I tend to use is the external deadline, regardless of whether it's my primary goal or just a marker in time. I'm frequently applying for art grants—not because I actually believe I have a shot of winning, but because those deadlines force me to take some time to reflect on and write about my work. Similarly, I almost always agree to speaking engagements because avoiding public embarrassment is a surefire way to force myself to pull together a cogent presentation on a topic that remains messy and unformed in my head.

How do designers get past the urge for perfection before they ship a product to the public for feedback?

Perfectionism is an extremely difficult habit to break, and admittedly, this is one of my greatest struggles, but if there's anything I've learned as much from my personal life as from my career, it's that feedback trumps all.

Knowing what doesn't work is equally as, if not more, valuable as knowing what does because it's actionable.

What is one failure you're thankful for?

Is it arrogant to say that I don't feel like I've actually had any failures? As cliché as it might sound, I look at everything as a learning opportunity. Have I put stuff out there that I'm less than pleased with? Absolutely. Have I let others down with my overcommitments and failure to deliver? Absolutely. I think I'm at least two weeks late with this interview.

Hipster Emblems, Hand-Crafted Axe

Joe Gebbia | Cofounder, Airbnb | San Francisco, CA

Conference Room, Airbnb Headquarters; Photo, Airbnb

"There's something fascinating about creating
something out of nothing."

Joe Gebbia

Solve Your Own Problems

Joe Gebbia aims high and learns from the ups and downs. He double majored in industrial and graphic design at Rhode Island School of Design (RISD), where he learned design skills, design thinking and the basics of entrepreneurship.

From his first entrepreneurial venture — starting RISD's basketball team — to cofounding Airbnb, a service that shares what's inspiring about every person and every home, in every country — Joe takes advantage of opportunities in front of him and solves problems that he experiences. Whether your next venture is starting a basketball team or launching the next great startup, you'll learn from and be inspired by Joe's perseverance and dedication.

How did you get into design?

I've been enthralled with the creative aspects of art, drawing and painting since I was a kid. During high school, teachers pulled my parents aside and told them to make sure I was exposed to as many art classes as possible. I've talked to many people whose interest in art was silenced because their parents didn't believe in artistic endeavors as a career. I'm really thankful for my parents' support.

During high school, I was admitted to the Georgia Governor's Honors Program for art. As a sophomore in high school, I got to spend six weeks in a summer program on a college campus. Looking back, that was a critical moment for the projection of my career; that's when I decided that I wanted to go to art school and study painting — of all things. I was motivated by the idea to create something that was so significant and visually arresting or innovative and different that art historians would have to put me in an art history book for future artists to discover. When I got to RISD, I discovered that they offered many other creative disciplines beyond painting, such as industrial and furniture design. I was captivated. I learned about designers such as Charles and Ray Eames, and I started to see a new way to apply creativity. I was on this path to becoming a painter; I had this vision of myself in the New York art scene, and in galleries and exhibitions worldwide, but I started to see a different path through the lens of the Eames. Their mantra was, 'Create the best for the most for the least.' Make the best design, for the most people, for the least price. The more I learned about them and their studio, the more I saw how creativity could be applied to design problems, and how through industrial design and manufacturing, good design could touch millions of lives. I was fascinated and saw design as an authentic way to express myself. The Eames' desire to do things that could touch millions of lives, and my desire to do something that would one day make the history books collided together in a passion for design.

I completed a double major in industrial design and graphic design. Little did I know, the workload of two degrees was training me for a startup one day. Designwise, it was the perfect merging of two worlds: visual communication, 2-D print, and interface design at a tactile and material level. I understood UX design through the lens of a flat world and a 3-D world. I learned to answer questions such as, 'How does this thing work, and how does it solve a design problem? And, 'How do you actually manufacture, build and sell in a market?' Learning 2-D and 3-D design in parallel helped round out a holistic design perspective. I saw how an idea is communicated, but also how it's translated into production. At the same time that I was learning about design, I founded my first startup. My first startup wasn't a business, and it wasn't a product — it was a sports team — the RISD basketball team.

I love basketball. It's a big part of my life. When I got to RISD, I asked, 'How do I sign up for the basketball team?' They said, 'We don't have one.' But they told me I could start one, so I paused for a minute not knowing what I was getting into and said, 'Sure, I'll start one.' Famous last words. I began the adventure of creating a sports team. Little by little I figured out how to make it happen. As it turns out, starting a sports team follows the same steps as a startup. I had to put a team together, raise money from the student government, and take care of operations and logistics. I had to create the season schedule, sell our team to other coaches so they would play us, and I had to create a brand — from the name, to the uniforms, to the signage. The hardest part of the challenge was something I never considered: 'How do you get art students to come out and support a sporting event on a Friday night?' It was an impossible task. But we figured it out after a lot of trial and error. People live for experiences, so that's what we created with our games.

All of the lessons learned from starting something from scratch taught me how to learn from mistakes. I also learned that I really enjoyed doing it. It was a lot of work, but I loved it. You're inventing. There's something fascinating about creating something out of nothing. It's like modern day alchemy.

RISD was great, both in the academic sense — learning the skills and the ways of thinking from a design point of view — but it was also great in the sense of learning the basics of entrepreneurship. I credit much of my success to my RISD education.

You met Brian Chesky at RISD?
Yes, I met Brian at RISD. He also studied industrial design, and we had classes together. Brian was the kind of guy who challenged me. When we were together, we would rate each other's game. We would make each other better at whatever we were trying to accomplish. He challenged me, and I challenged him in ways that I hadn't experienced from many other people in my life. After a couple years, it became apparent to me that one day we would start a company together. I had a premonition. One day before we graduated, I invited him out for pizza, and I told him that I felt like we were going to start a business together one day, and there would be books written about it.

What was your path in between graduating school and cofounding Airbnb?

Design school is a safe place to stretch your brain. And stretch it again. And go to these far corners of the creative universe because you can. There are no consequences; you can do whatever you want. It's intentional, and they create space for that because it encourages wild thinking. You're not afforded that all of the time in the real world. After five years on campus, I was ready for a real-world project. I started my first business the day after graduation.

The product was based on an idea I had as a freshman. As a first-year student, you take foundation courses and end up in critiques for what feels like eight hours a day. The studios themselves are great for making art, but they are less great for sitting around critiquing art. Picture these uncomfortable metal stools and wooden floors. The studios were covered in paint and charcoal dust. The materials rubbed off onto the seat of your pants, so at the end of the day, when we stood up, everyone had this ridiculous bun print on the seat of their pants. I came up with the idea of a seat cushion called CritBuns. It would be comfortable, clean and you could sit on it during a crit. I drew a little sketch, but I had no idea how to make a product as a freshman. During senior year, after completing the industrial design program, I had a very good idea of how to make a product. At RISD, graduates receive a paper diploma, but they also receive a unique gift called a 'design diploma.' Students submit design ideas, and RISD pays for the development costs of the chosen design diploma.

I submitted my idea for CritBuns, and it won. They told me on May 1, four weeks before graduation. On top of two degree projects, I had to figure out how to get 800 CritBuns manufactured and delivered to Providence in four weeks. All I had was a dinky prototype and the 3-D file. This was another lesson in startup hustle. I did a Google search and called every

RISD Balls, Basketball Team Logo

manufacturer on the first 20 pages of results. I told them what I needed, and they laughed — they said it would take 12 weeks just to get the mold made. Two weeks passed, and the school called me every day wondering if they needed to order a backup. I thought all of my options were exhausted; then I realized that I never asked the guy who ran the metal shop whether he had any contacts. He had a guy he thought could do it, so I called him and poured my heart out. He said, 'Joe, I feel you, and I sense your passion. I can move some projects around and have the metal mold to you in three days.' My jaw dropped. And I learned a life lesson in perseverance.

Two weeks later, 400 red and 400 blue CritBuns with 'RISD class of '05' screen printed on the top showed up the day before graduation. It was such a rush. I didn't get paid, but the school gave me the mold afterward. The biggest capital expense for CritBuns was handed to me, so I started my company right away. I spent the summer building out the product, applying design thinking and marketing, and filing for a patent — I took a different path than most of my friends. I went back to RISD and said, 'What if we gave the incoming class CritBuns as a welcome to RISD gift. They loved it, I had my first real order, and I was able to manufacture some inventory for myself. I'll never forget the day when my first order [outside the school] came in, and I had 400 or 500 CritBuns in my basement. I thought shit, 'Now I have to go out there and sell these.' I started going door-to-door in Providence trying to sell them. I went business-to-business. The first four or five people rejected them. It was heartbreaking. I put all this time and love into this project, and people didn't want to buy it. I remembered this equation that I heard once from a professor at Brown University. It's an equation that's gotten me through a lot of rejection. The equation is SW squared (x) WC = MO. It means Some Won't + Some Will (x) Who Cares = Move On.

CritBuns, Top View

Some people are going to love your product; some people aren't going to love your product. But you have to keep going. I thought about that every time I got rejected. I'll never forget the first store that bought four CritBuns in Providence. For the first time, I saw the process of how a concept that started in my head got all the way to the shelf in a store. After that, I had all the confidence in the world. CritBuns got international distribution and was exhibited all over the world. The biggest accomplishment was selling them at the MoMA store in New York City.

Did you take some of that confidence and lessons learned to Airbnb when you were getting started?
Yes, definitely. It prepared me emotionally for what was to come. There were a lot of highs and lows with CritBuns, but the scale of the highs and lows was pretty small. Airbnb has had the greatest successes and the worst failures you can imagine. It stretched the emotional capacity of the entire team. With Airbnb, I dealt with the same emotions as I did with CritBuns, but it was much more extreme.

How was the feedback when you and Brian pitched Airbnb as two designers? How did you find your CTO?
Brian and I were savvy enough to know we'd need a technical person to make it work. Nate Blecharczyk, Airbnb's CTO, was my roommate in San Francisco before Brian. Nate and I would work in the apartment all weekend on side projects. We'd work until 3 or 4 in the morning on a Saturday, and our third roommate, who was more of a corporate guy, would come stumbling in at 3 a.m. It was then that I realized Nate and I shared a common work ethic. I made a mental note that if I ever needed to work with a developer in the future, that it would be Nate. That's how we built the team. Since college, anytime I've come across someone who is

special or stands out to me, I make a mental note, catalogue them in my mind, and tell myself if we ever need that type of person in the future, I'm going to find them. A lot of the people on our team are people I met six or eight years ago and flagged them in my mind. Nate is one of those special people. A hundred things have fallen into place in the last four years, and Nate is one of them.

When he joined the team, he liked our idea of bridging the online and offline, and we all set out to build a new version of our site. At the time, we thought the big opportunity was in the need for housing during conferences. We were working with this 'event-space' model and built a new version of the site for the 2008 SXSW. It was just a listing service with no payment or reputation system yet. We had 20 or so people list spaces but only two or three reservations, and we were one of them.

We learned a profound lesson in Austin. Our host picked us up from the airport and had our beds laid out in the living room with towels and mints on the pillows. He cooked us dinner, and it was an amazing experience—until he asked us for money. The whole exchange was so awkward that it ruined the great part of the experience. We decided we had to remove any awkward experiences for this thing to work. If you can pay for a hotel room online, we knew we had to bring payment online. There were no sites doing that for a personal apartment. We decided to do it on the spot, so people could use a credit card and not have to talk about money with their host. SXSW also helped us realize that we were so focused on the event model that we were missing the big picture. People emailed us and asked how to use our site if they traveled to London or Brazil and there were no events happening. They couldn't. We scrapped the event focus and decided to create an open marketplace for travel around the world. We spent the summer of 2008 building out this new vision, from the ground up.

In the course of building a two-sided marketplace, we realized how hard it was to appeal to both guests and hosts at the same time. You can have a good-looking store, but if there are no products on the shelf, no one will come to your store. We had to figure out how to get people to list their spaces online.

That same summer, everyone was talking about Barack Obama, so we started to look ahead to the Democratic National Convention in Denver. There were all these amazing stories in the press about the housing shortage in Denver. We decided we'd launch in time for that and ride the coattails of the Obama campaign. Sure enough, it worked. We went from zero to 800 listings in four weeks. It started with local bloggers and ended up with international coverage. We launched there, and we had this moment where everything was going awesome. We had this notion that if we built it they would come. But it's not true. If you build it, they will not come. Promptly after, the DNC things plummeted, and our business went flat.

We entered what is known in Silicon Valley as the Trough of Sorrow. It exists after you launch—when the novelty has warn off, and you don't yet have a product-market fit because the assumptions that you've made are wrong. We had to go out and pitch investors. We needed to raise money to keep going. We got introductions to 20 investors. Ten of them returned our emails; five of them met us for coffee, and zero of them invested. We were deflated. We had done all of the work to build the site; we got a lot of press, but no one wanted to invest because they thought our idea was crazy. They couldn't wrap their heads around how a stranger was going to stay in another stranger's home. It also didn't help that we were predominately a nontechnical team. Investors didn't recognize the value of designers, and it was actually a liability to have designer founders. We bucked the model. Traditional startup founding teams were composed of engineers and maybe someone with an MBA, not crazy right-brained people who design things. Thank god we had Nate. Then the market crashed, and all investment went silent. We were in a tough spot. We had 10 grand in credit-card debt, with no investment; law firms laughed us out of conference rooms; we had no users; there was no traffic on the site, and our parents thought we were crazy. It was very bleak for us. I would call this rock bottom. The only thing that got us through was thinking back to the amazing experience we had with three guests in our apartment. We always returned to that moment hosting our friends Michael, Amol and Kate on airbeds, and socializing with them during their stay. We weren't going to give up until we could make that work for other people, too.

In the fall of 2008, we applied to Y Combinator. We had a 10-minute interview with YC's cofounder Paul Graham that felt like an interrogation. As we were leaving, I gave him a box of Obama O's—the promotion piece we created for the DNC in which we bought a bulk supply of generic cereal and created brands for Barack Obama and John McCain. He said, 'Did you buy these for me?' I said, 'No, we made them.' I told him how Obama O's sold out and how we netted the funds we needed to keep Airbnb alive. He immediately put the box on the shelf behind his desk. We got into Y Combinator.

He told us later that he didn't believe in us because of our crazy idea for Airbnb but that he believed in us because of the Obama O's. He said, 'If you can figure out how to sell a box of cereal for $40, I'm sure you can figure out how to make your website work.' I like to say that Obama got us into Y Combinator. Without Y Combinator, we wouldn't be having this conversation about Airbnb. It was there that we figured out what was wrong with our product and how to make it better. We tapped into our design abilities and incorporated practices from industrial design. When you design a product for a consumer—shoes, a chair, a phone or a medical product—you start by becoming the consumer. Empathy inspires new ideas. For us, the notion hadn't yet occurred to us because we felt a divide between the industrial design and technology worlds. The Internet startup world's convention of thinking is that you need to solve problems in a scalable way. You need to solve problems with lines of code, and the Internet allows you to do that. The same line of code can touch one user or 10,000 users. But, as soon as we started to do things that didn't scale, everything started to click. When we let ourselves think like industrial designers, we began to make a better product that people started to use. We traveled to NYC; we talked to hosts; we did unofficial ethnographic research. We observed people using Airbnb. We experienced all of the pain points firsthand. Until that point, we thought about how to make things better in scalable ways, but we needed to experience it for ourselves. Paul Graham gave us permission to do things that didn't scale. We came back to our roots and applied the industrial design process to the Internet—merging customer feedback with our obsession for good design. Once we did that, everything clicked, and we began making money rapidly. The numbers started going so quickly that we started to get inbound requests from investors. We raised some money to build out our team and haven't looked back since.

Now, many years and with a very talented team, we've reached a scale of millions of people to the point we're thinking through the design of a new economy. The movement has been labeled 'the sharing economy' or 'collaborative consumption.' It's an economy powered by people sharing what they have with someone who wants it, made possible for the first time in our history by a mature Internet and a billion-plus mobile devices. It's the beginning of something much bigger; perhaps this is the same feeling the industrialists had when the

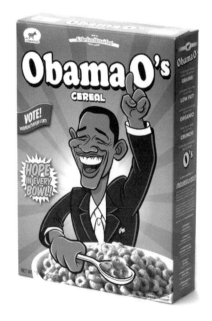

Obama O's, Promotional Piece

Airbnb, Loft in the Heart of New York City; Photo, Airbnb

industrial revolution was just beginning more than 100 years ago. I believe the age of mass manufacture is behind us, and a more personal, local and resourceful way of consuming is ahead of us. I see it unfolding at a global scale every day.

Have the tech and business industries changed their perception of designers?
Absolutely. I'd like to think it's in part because of us. I know the investment community has changed because of us and others. That is one of the many contributions that I feel we've been able to make. I'm really proud of that.

We were able to prove some people wrong and show them a different way of doing things. RISD taught me how to do that. Yes, two art school guys can run a successful company. Now, some of our investors look for designers. Paul Graham said that he now looks for designers. I think we've opened up people's minds to the idea of designer founders. There are groups such as the Designer Fund that didn't exist when we started. We've opened a path for designers to follow. We're not the only ones.

We followed pioneers, too. But I hope it comes across that we're just like other designers who were complete outsiders to an industry, who faced uncomfortable amounts of rejection and lacked every imaginable resource, other than our creativity and hustle. Here's to inspiring the next designer out there.

Notes

Resources

The following is a list of resources that are mentioned throughout this book. Use them as a source of inspiration, education and as places to learn through the process of discovery.

52 Weeks of UX
52 Weeks of UX is a year's worth of weekly posts about user experience design.
52weeksofux.com

500 Startups
500 Startups is an early stage startup accelerator program based in Silicon Valley.
500.co

Best Made Company
Best Made Company is a product company that empowers people to get outside, use their hands and in doing so embark on a life of fulfilling project and lasting experiences.
bestmadeco.com

Brand New
Brand New is a blog that chronicles and provides opinions on corporate and brand identity design.
underconsideration.com/brandnew

Brooklyn Beta
Brooklyn Beta is a web conference, founded by Cameron Koczon and Chris Shiflett, that's aimed at the "work hard and be nice to people crowd."
brooklynbeta.org

Build Conference

The Build Conference is a week-long festival of people who design for the web in Belfast, UK.
buildconf.com

Buy A Pair, Give A Pair

Buy A Pair, Give A Pair is a program by Warby Parker that gives away a pair of glasses for each one that it sells.
warbyparker.com/do-good

CoTweet

CoTweet is a web-based platform to manage multiple users and multiple Twitter accounts.
cotweet.com

CodePen

CodePen is a playground for HTML, CSS and JavaScript.
codepen.io

Collaborative Fund

Collaborative Fund is a venture fund that aims to be the leading source of capital and strategic support for creative entrepreneurs who want to change the world.
collaborativefund.com

Cosmonaut

The cosmonaut is a wide-grip stylus for touch screens created by Studio Neat.
studioneat.com/products/cosmonaut

Coudal Partners

Coudal Partners is an advertising, design and interactive firm located in Chicago and run by Jim Coudal, who partnered with Aaron Draplin to produce Field Notes.
coudal.com

CreativeMornings

CreativeMornings is a monthly and global breakfast lecture series started by Tina Roth Eisenberg.
creativemornings.com

CritBuns

CritBuns is a company, started by Airbnb's Joe Gebbia, that makes portable foam seat cushions.
critbuns.com

CSS-Tricks

CSS-Tricks is a CSS resource designed, developed and run by Chris Coyier.
css-tricks.com

Digging Into WordPress
Digging Into WordPress is a book about WordPress development written by Jeff Starr and Chris Coyier.
digwp.com

Don't Fear the Internet
Don't Fear the Internet is a website that teaches basic HTML and CSS to non-web designers and is run by Jessica Hische and Russ Maschmeyer.
dontfeartheinternet.com

Done Not Done
Done Not Done, created by Fictive Kin, is a to-do list for things you want to do, not the things you have to do.
donenotdone.com

Dribbble
Dribbble is a show-and-tell platform for designers, who share small screenshots of the designs and applications they're working on.
dribbble.com

Eli, No!
Eli, No! is an illustrated children's book by Katie Kirk about her dog, Eli.
eighthourday.com/work/eli-no-childrens-book

Etsy
Etsy is a social commerce platform that enables its users to buy and sell handmade items.
etsy.com

Fictive Kin
Fictive Kin is a group of good people making good work.
fictivekin.com

Field Notes Brand
Field Notes is a product line of memo books and other goods made by Aaron Draplin in partnership with Jim Coudal.
fieldnotesbrand.com

Frank
Frank is a beautifully branded hot dog restaurant, co-owned by Christian Helms, in Austin, Texas.
hotdogscoldbeer.com

Freelance Ain't Free
Freelance Ain't Free is a side project and product line started by Mikey Burton.
freelanceaintfree.com

General Assembly

General Assembly transforms thinkers into creators through education and opportunities in technology, business and design.
generalassemb.ly

Inker Linker

Inker Linker is a side project by Jessica Hische that allows users to find a printer based on what's most important to them and what printers do best.
inkerlinker.com

Insites: The Book

Insites: The Book is a book of stories about designers by Elliot Jay Stocks.
shop.viewportindustries.com/products/insites-the-book

Keenan Cummings

Keenan Cummings is a product designer, cofounder of Wander and author of the foreword to this book.
keenancummings.com

Kickstarter

Kickstarter is a funding platform for creative projects — everything from films, games and music to art, design and technology.
kickstarter.com

Leroy C.

Leroy C. is a vinyl toy created by Invisible Creature for Super7's "Monster Family" series.
invisiblecreature.com/shop/toys

Lost Type Co-op

Lost Type Co-op is a font foundry that allows users to pay what they want and is the first of its kind.
lostype.com

Obsessive Consumption

Obsessive Consumption is a project by Kate Bingaman-Burt based on a series of drawings of her daily purchases.
katebingamanburt.com/obsess

Paul Graham

Paul Graham is the cofounder of Y Combinator, programmer and essayist.
paulgraham.com

Pilot & Captain

Pilot & Captain is a product line about the good old days of planes, trains and discovery, created by The Heads of State.
pilotandcaptain.com

Rushmore

Rushmore is a web platform that makes it easier to be a music fan, or a music artist.
rushmore.fm

Sad Santa

Sad Santa is a children's book about Santa's post-holiday blues, by Tad Carpenter.
sadsantabook.com

Sasquatch! Music Festival

Sasquatch! Music Festival is a four-day music festival on Memorial Day Weekend at the scenic Gorge in central Washington state.
sasquatchfestival.com

Seesaw

Seesaw is a social application that lets you get opinions from friends when you need them most. Cofounded by Kyle Sollenberger.
seesaw.co

ShopTalk

ShopTalk is a podcast about all things web design and development, hosted by Dave Rupert and Chris Coyier.
shoptalkshow.com

Standard Grit

Standard Grit makes handmade, limited-edition textiles crafted in the South.
standardgrit.com

Studiomates

Studiomates is a collaborative workspace of designers, illustrators, bloggers, writers and developers.
studiomates.com

Svpply

Svpply is a curated collection of the world's best products and stores.
svpply.com

SwissMiss

SwissMiss is a design blog and studio run by Tina Roth Eisenberg.
swiss-miss.com

TeuxDeux

TeuxDeux is a simple, design to-do app created by Cameron Koczon and Tina Roth Eisenberg.
teuxdeux.com

The Daily Drop Cap
The Daily Drop Cap is a side project by Jessica Hische that features illustrative initial caps. dailydropcap.com

The Designer Fund
The Designer Fund is a community of designers who invest in designer founders through mentorship, funding and access to their networks. designerfund.com

The Manual
The Manual is a multivolume series of books that use the maturing of the discipline of web design as a starting point for deeper explorations of our work and who we are as designers. Published by Andy McMillan. alwaysreadthemanual.com

Thinking for a Living
Thinking for a Living is a curated blog of thought-provoking design content run by Duane King. thinkingforaliving.org

TikTok+LunaTik
TikTok+LunaTik are watch kits designed by Scott Wilson and funded on Kickstarter. lunatik.com

Title Case
Title Case is the studio office of Jessica Hische and Erik Marinovich in San Francisco, Calif. titlecase.co

UnderConsideration
UnderConsideration is a graphic design enterprise by Armin Vit and Bryony Gomez-Palacio that runs a network of blogs, publishes books, organizes live events and judged competitions. underconsideration.com

Viewport Industries
Viewport Industries is Elliot Jay Stocks' and Keir Whitaker's creative partnership. viewportindustries.com

XOXO Conference
XOXO Conference is an arts and technology festival celebrating disruptive creativity, run by Andy McMillan. xoxofest.com

Y Combinator
Y Combinator provides seed-stage funding to startups and is located in Silicon Valley. ycombinator.com

Design Entrepreneurs

Aaron Draplin
draplin.com
@draplin

Andy McMillan
fiction.co
@andymcmillan

Armin Vit
underconsideration.com
@ucllc

Ben Pieratt
pieratt.com
@pieratt

Cameron Koczon
fictivecameron.com
@FictiveCameron

Chris Coyier
chriscoyier.net
@chriscoyier

Christian Helms
helmsworkshop.com
@xianhelms

Dan Provost
studioneat.com
@studioneat

Don Clark
invisiblecreature.com
@icreature

Duane King
kingduane.com
@DuaneKing

Dusty Summers
theheadsofstate.com
@TheHeadsofState

Elliot Jay Stocks
elliotjaystocks.com
@elliotjaystocks

Enrique Allen
designerfund.com
@EnriqueAllen

Jake Nickell
jakenickell.com
@skaw

Jen Bilik
knockknockstuff.com
@knockknock

Jessica Hische
jessicahische.is
@jessicahische

Joe Gebbia
joegebbia.com
@jgebbia

Josh Brewer
jbrewer.me
@jbrewer

Kate Bingaman-Burt
katebingamanburt.com
@katebingburt

Katie Kirk
eighthourday.com
@EightHourDay

Kyle Sollenberger
kylesollenberger.com
@kyle

Mikey Burton
mikeyburton.com
@mikeyburton

Mimi O Chun
long-winded.tumblr.com
@mimiochun

Neil Blumenthal
warbyparker.com
@WarbyParker

Peter Buchanan-Smith
bestmadeco.com
@BestMadeCo

Randy J. Hunt
randyjhunt.com
@randyjhunt

Riley Cran
rileycran.com
@rileycran

Scott Wilson
mnml.com
@ScottWilsonID

Tad Carpenter
tadcarpenter.com
@TadCarpenter

Wilson Miner
wilsonminer.com
@wilsonminer

Illustrators

Brent Couchman
brentcouchman.com
@brentcouchman

Dana Steffe
danasteffe.com
@dana_steffe

Ed Nacional
ednacional.com
@ednacional

Eric R. Mortensen
ericrmortensen.com
@EricRMortensen

Invisible Creature
invisiblecreature.com
@icreature

Matt Stevens
hellomattstevens.com
@MattStevensCLT

Mikey Burton
mikeyburton.com
@mikeyburton

Nate Utesch
nthnl.com
@nateutesch

Riley Cran
rileycran.com
@rileycran

Scotty Reifsnyder
seescotty.com
@SeeScotty

Tad Carpenter
tadcarpenter.com
@TadCarpenter

The Heads Of State
theheadsofstate.com
@TheHeadsofState

Acknowledgements

This book would not be possible without the incredible support of our families, friends, mentors and Kickstarter supporters. To all of those who have taught us so much throughout the last year — many of whom gave their knowledge and time without expecting anything in return. Thank you.

To our classmates and professors at Maryland Institute College of Art, where Kern and Burn began as our MFA thesis project. Ellen Lupton, Jennifer Cole Phillips and David Barringer taught us well, and encouraged us to pursue great design and excellent content. Our incredible classmates challenged us every day to work hard and be good people. We miss you all. Thank you.

To Eric R. Mortensen for designing the Kern and Burn icon set and an illustration for this book, and for supplying us with a workspace in Brooklyn and setting an incredibly high bar for us to chase. But more than that — for being an amazing friend to us both. Thank you.

To Krissi Xenakis for being a constant sounding board, loyal friend, host mom and provider of balance. You are our hero. Thank you.

To Allison Loerch for taking on the incredibly difficult assignment of editing our words and our book. You went above and beyond, and we are lucky. Thank you.

To the design entrepreneurs and illustrators in this book, who shared their perspectives with our readers through words and imagery, we are forever grateful. Thank you.

To the design entrepreneurs who graciously took time to answer questions for our blog, 100 Days of Design Entrepreneurship: Alissa Walker, Allan Chochinov, Andrew Losowsky, Charles Adler, Chris Muccioli, Craig Welsh, Danny Miller, Elana Schlenker, Frank Chimero, House Industries, Keetra Dean Dixon, Khoi Vinh, Public School and Tymn Armstrong. Thank you.

Finally, to all of you who kern and burn, and who embrace the risk of failure daily. This book is for you, but also inspired by you. Thank you.

Kickstarter Backers

We owe the success of our Kickstarter campaign to our dedicated, enthusiastic and encouraging readers in the design and entrepreneurial communities. The Kickstarter platform has allowed us to share the journey and reward of creating something meaningful, together.

Craig Welsh
James Ramsay
Kneadle
Maktoum Saeed Almaktoum
Matt Hoover
Nick Setthachayanon
Scott Hatch
Susan J. Ganz
Tom and Jeanne Heltzel

Alec Perkins
Andy McMillan
Astro Studios
Ben Blumenfeld
Carl and DebbiSue Hoover
Christine Kim Brueck
Christopher Clark
Dave Hoffer
Delve Withrington
Douglas W. Timmermeyer
Dustin Leer
Ellen Lupton
Enrique Allen

Jason Chen
Jason Gottlieb
Jed and Laura Burkholder
Jenifer Bailey
Jonathan Stephens
Justin Mezzell
Ken Hejduk
Laura Nephew Guzi
Lauren A. Thomas
M. Vennelin
Michael Frederick
Michal Kopec
Oscar Palmér
Robert Brown
Rory Keohane
Scott Stowell
Scott Wilson + (MNML)
Silas Crews
Steven R. Bible
The Infantree
The Karle Family
Thomas Hill
Thank you.

Sponsors

We would like to thank the following companies for their generosity and support of our book. Shopify, Squarespace and MailChimp are all products that help designers take their careers into their own hands and share what they love.

Shopify
Shopify is a powerful ecommerce-website solution that allows you to sell online by providing everything you need to create an online store.
shopify.com

Squarespace
Squarespace is the easiest way for anyone to create an exceptional website. Pages, galleries, blogs, domains, hosting, analytics and 24/7 support are all included.
squarespace.com

MailChimp
MailChimp helps you design email newsletters, share them on social networks, integrate with services you already use, and track your results. It's like your own personal publishing platform.
mailchimp.com

MailChimp

Introduction Notes

Silicon Valley. Dir. Randall MacLowry. WGBH   15
Educational Foundation, 2013. Film.

Berlin, Leslie. *The Man Behind the Microchip:*   15
Robert Noyce and the Invention of Silicon
Valley. New York: Oxford University Press, 2005.
Print.

Deresiewicz, William. "Generation Sell," The   16
New York Times, November 2011. <http://www.
nytimes.com/2011/11/13/opinion/sunday/
the-entrepreneurial-generation.
html?pagewanted=all&_r=0>.

Pieratt, Ben. "Dear Graphic and Web Designers,   16
please understand that there are greater
opportunities available to you." 2012. <http://
blog.pieratt.com/post/7537191978/dear-graphic-
and-web-designers-please-understand-that>.

Safian, Robert. "This Is Generation Flux: Meet   16
The Pioneers Of The New (And Chaotic)
Frontier Of Business." *Fast Company*, January
2012. <http://www.fastcompany.com/1802732/
generation-flux-meet-pioneers-new-and-
chaotic-frontier-business>.

About the Authors

Tim Hoover

Tim Hoover is a freelance designer and writer living and working in Brooklyn. He is the cofounder of Kern and Burn, and The People's Pennant, and former partner at The Infantree. He received his MFA in Graphic Design from the Maryland Institute College of Art (MICA). He's quasi-Amish, and overly certain he's on the verge of starting a really-disruptive-and-valuable company.
iamtimhoover.com
@iamtimhoover

Jessica Karle Heltzel

Jessica Karle Heltzel is a designer and writer living and working in New York. She is the cofounder of Kern and Burn, and The People's Pennant. She received her MFA in Graphic Design from the Maryland Institute College of Art (MICA). She works as a designer for General Assembly and often can be spotted carrying 14 bags through the streets of Manhattan.
jkheltzel.com
@jkheltzel